ENLIGHTENING MOMENTS

MOMENTS

Living Beyond the Frustration Cycle

GARY AND RADHA BELLO

PACIFIC HORIZON
CONSULTING
ILLUMINATE SOLUTIONS.
NAVIGATE LIFE.

The information contained in this book is based upon the research and personal and professional experiences of the authors. It is not intended as a substitute for consulting with a healthcare practitioner. The teachings in this book are recommended as an adjunct to any therapeutic treatments the reader is currently undergoing or in which he or she is currently participating. Should the reader have any questions concerning the appropriateness of any of the exercises or methods described in this book, the authors strongly suggest consulting a professional healthcare advisor.

The client examples used in this book are composite stories. Actual names and identifying characteristics have not been used, and any resemblance to a specific individual is coincidental.

Pacific Horizon Consulting
www.pacifichorizonconsulting.com

1131 SE 4th Street #106
Boynton Beach, FL 33435

3680 Point Grey Road
Vancouver BC V6R 1A9

ISBN-13: 978-06155266-2-1
ISBN-10: 06155266-2-4

Typesetting/Book design/Cover design:
Gary A. Rosenberg • TheBookCouple.com

Contents

To all of the knowledgeable teachers in our life.
Our intention is to remain true to the wisdom you have
shared with us over the past forty years.

It's not what you look at in life that matters,
it's what you see.

—HENRY DAVID THOREAU

A Note from the Authors

The program introduced in this book is intended to lead you toward greater ease in your relationships with yourself, others, and the world around you by increasing your level of awareness in all areas of your life. Through this increased awareness, you will be more available for the many opportunities life has to offer. However, this program does require a firm commitment from you to closely examine how you operate, including your concepts about yourself, your beliefs, and especially your tendency to react or respond to the challenging events that present themselves to you on a daily basis.

If you approach this program with honesty, you may discover things that cause you to feel some discomfort. Know that feeling this discomfort is an important part of the process, and approach these feelings with curiosity, courage, and compassion. It is only through facing and feeling our discomforts with enhanced awareness that we can completely move out of old patterns and clear the way for more confidence, acceptance, satisfaction, and joy in our lives, both professionally and personally.

Editor's note: While this book is written from Gary's perspective and in his voice, the teachings and philosophies in the book reflect both Gary and Radha's combined work over the course of forty years.

Acknowledgments

The magnificence of a tree can be measured by the abundance of its fruit. And the tree of life has been generous in showering us with teachers, coaches, therapists, friends, clients, and students who directly assisted us in the research, analysis, writing, editing, proof-reading, design, layout, and support that went into the birthing of this book.

We start by thanking our very first guru and yoga teacher, Swami Satchidananda, whose Integral Yoga taught us the ancient truths of India in a practical and relevant manner. A few years later we were introduced to Ron Kurtz, the originator of Hakomi Therapy, by our two friends Dyrian and Devi. All three of these individuals were instrumental in showing us how to integrate our yoga studies with a body-centered approach to psychotherapy.

During my early years studying and teaching in Montreal, I had the good fortune of meeting a bright, funny, and intelligent person whom I asked for assistance when we were creating our first newsletter. Allan Hirsh's cartoon creations were a big hit, and forty years later, he is our dear friend as well as a gifted artist, cartoonist, psychotherapist, and delightful caring human being. We are thrilled to include his cartoons in this book.

After leaving Montreal we began our studies with a wild and crazy swami living in the Himalayas. His knowledge of raja yoga (the study of mind and the practice of meditation) allowed us to both understand and experience the deeper states of consciousness that exist beyond the material world.

We would not have reached this point in our career if it were not for our community in South Florida. These dedicated individuals enabled us to develop our relationship tools and concepts. Thank you Alice, Anastasia, Anthony, Bruce, Carolyn, Sherry, Patricia, Teresa, Richard, Doug, Michael, Vincent, Dana, Sheri, Drew, Joan, Jack, Karen, Kim, Luke, Lauren, Mel, Nathan, Rachel, Sheila, Sondra, and many others.

We thank Carlee for the many long days and nights she lent a helping hand, and to Jeremy, who as the coauthor of our next book *The Swami and the Married Woman* typed feverishly as I paced back and forth excitedly dictating my thoughts.

To Stephen Placido. We appreciate how he was able to take the ideas presented in this book, integrate them into his life, and as our first enlightening moments trainer proved to us that the concepts stood alone in their ability to transform people's lives.

We are so delighted to have The Book Couple, Carol and Gary Rosenberg, on our team. Carol, an accomplished book editor and writer who has worked with many top publishers, is literally the talent behind the words in this book. And Gary, her partner, is a creative book designer and layout specialist, who infused every page of this work with his creativity.

As we struggled to come up with an acronym for our five-step process, our dear friends Ray and Jack Resels stepped up to help. They had already spent many long hours assisting us in the fine-tuning of our concepts, but when they suggested we use GRACE, we were delighted. Our assistant, Rachel Martens, was the creative magic behind the design of the Frustration Cycle and Exiting The Frustration Cycle. We are also extremely grateful to our CEO, Rachel Greenfeld. We appreciate all of her skill at taking this book and our company, Pacific Horizon Consulting, into the professional arena.

We would like to acknowledge our dear friend and teacher Jeffrey Armstrong, who for the past forty years has been studying and teaching the Vedas—the ancient wisdom of India. The time he spent editing and fine-tuning this work and writing the foreword was invaluable to the success of this project. Since our relationship tools and concepts are based on the Vedic teachings, we were blessed to have an author of many books, a poet, a *jotish* (Vedic astrologer), and one of the most knowledgeable scholars of the Vedas in the world assisting us.

We feel a tremendous amount of gratitude to our friend and client Steve. His assistance and encouragement were the most important factors in making this new chapter of our life possible.

Thanks to my cousin Joey for being the inspiration behind the theme of the entire book: *the journey begins with awareness.*

And finally we thank the *creative intelligence of the universe* for the wonder, awe, and inspiration that has taught us to appreciate each and every moment of our life. We attribute any benefit that you may receive from this book to the fact that we are merely students on a journey, and the entire universe is our teacher.

Foreword
by Jeffrey Armstrong/Kavindra Rishi

This important book is on the leading edge of a revolution in psychology and the psyche of Western civilization. It is living proof that Kipling was wrong. East and West have not only met, they have dated, gotten engaged, married, and are now having children. Gary (Gopal) Bello is a new branch of two trees: Western Psychology descending through Sigmund Freud, his student Wilhelm Reich, and Ron Kurtz has been grafted to the ancient Banyan tree of Patanjali's Ashtanga Yoga from the Himalayas in India. The result is a new/old, modern/ancient—but decidedly timeless—approach to the human psyche. This book is revolutionary—it will change the way you live, and most important, the way you solve life's problems.

The transfer of knowledge from India has been going on for thousands of years, but—mostly for political reasons—remained underground below the social radar. For example, it is a well-known fact that the Greek philosopher Pythagoras (*Pitta Gurus* in Sanskrit) went to India and studied Yoga and Indian philosophy. When he returned to Greece around 700 BC, he was vegetarian and taught an entirely new perspective. Two hundred years later, his teachings shaped the thinking of Socrates, whose famous student Plato influenced philosophy and religion for the next 2,500 years. The contemporary saying is, "Western philosophy is merely footnotes on Plato."

By the time of Christ, Rome was sending 150 ships per year to India, trading in spices and other luxury items. If you have ever listened to the words of Jesus in the New Testament and thought his message resembled that of Mahatma Gandhi, it is because the Middle East was as full of the knowledge of India during that period as California was in the 1960s. At that same time [in Christ's day], the University of Alexandria in Egypt housed the largest library outside of India and had many professors from both China and India. It was the UC Berkeley of its time, though this is not commonly known today.

Later, during the Dark Ages and medieval times in Europe, Egyptian, Indian, and Chinese knowledge was forced underground into numerous secret societies and, of necessity, hidden from the dangerous eyes of an inquisitional Catholic Church. By the fifteen century and, increasingly since then, Europe's contact with India through colonization started a steady stream of Indian knowledge flowing into the Western world through translations of the many texts in the Vedic library. The Germans took a keen interest in Indian knowledge. The philosopher Schopenhauer read the Vedic *Upanishads* daily. Germany has the largest Sanskrit library outside of India, which acted as a catalyst and source of material for German scientists and physicists of the twentieth century.

In England, William Blake and the Romantic Poets were deeply moved by many forms of Indian knowledge. In America, the so-called "American Transcendentalists," including Emerson, Thoreau, Parker, and Channing, transformed the Protestant Church into Unity, Unitarian, The Church of Religious Science, and many other similar groups by blending Indian philosophy—especially that of the *Bhagavad Gita*—with the views of Christianity. Even today, very few people realize how deeply India's knowledge shaped these historical developments. But the time of the acknowledgment of "borrowing from the East" was rapidly approaching.

In the last one hundred years, as psychology developed and branched into its many viewpoints, invisibly and without public notice Indian Philosophy began to show up everywhere. Abraham Maslow developed his *Theory of the Evolution* or *Hierarchy of Needs* based on the seven chakras of Indian yogic thinking. William Sheldon developed the three psychosomatic body types of ectomorph, mesomorph, and endomorph based on the Greek and Ayurvedic system of body types vata, pitta, and kapha. The Transpersonal Psychology movement was the direct outgrowth of Buddhist thought, another branch of the ancient knowledge of India. Stanislav Grof and his work with holotropic breathing are directly connected to *pranayama,* the advanced breathing technology of yoga. A myriad of other modalities exploring the fundamental premise of yoga and the mind/body connection have been and are on the cutting edge of both psychological and new medical modalities.

My own forty years of work—bringing the knowledge of India into English and the Western cultural framework—began with my exposure to the works of Carl Jung while I was getting a degree in Psychology. Jung visited India several times and while there developed his *Theory of Archetypes* and the concept of *Anima* and *Animas.* By the end of his career, he was known to say, "I can know more about a patient with a horoscope then with a stethoscope." Jung led an entire generation out of the narrow confines of Abrahamic religion and mechanistic science into a universal realm of ideas that are the common property of all cultures. Joseph Campbell's cross-cultural explorations of myth, his several visits to India and provocative commentary on their mystic stories further opened the minds of a whole generation to the importance of a Universal view of who we are or might be.

For example, George Lucas, a student of Campbell, took one of India's most famous epics—the *Ramayana*—combined it with the archetypes of Jung and *the heroes journey* of Campbell, and taught a whole generation about "the force" or vital life energy of the cosmos. In Japan, they call it "ki," in China "chi," in India "prana"—the intelligent living vitality that animates all existence. Before the final episode of *Star Wars* was even finished, Yoga was on its way to sweeping across the Western world. Over ten percent of North America is currently practicing Yoga. A hundred million people are meditating all around the world. Yoga is a bigger business than Microsoft, and is on its way to uniting all countries in the web of an ancient and venerable science of how to live sustainably on our planet. My own work with Distinctivist Vedanta, combined with the insights of AyurVedic astrology, has led me to create a new method of counselling that I call "Transcendental Personal Psychology." It is based on the yogic premise that we are eternal individuals, here within matter, learning to unleash our full potential and perfect our divine personhood.

Gary (Gopal) Bello's method of cultivating enlightening moments in all we do is one more great advance in making the unifying and peaceful wisdom of Yoga integrated and available to a world of over-stressed over-achievers, who are all very much in need of a new paradigm and new tools for sustainable living. They will find them in this breakthrough yogic/psychological work. In these pages, Radha and Gopal are inviting us to learn the ancient and sublime methods that have made India the home of enlightenment and cooperation for thousands of years. I hope you receive their grace and know that you will become your best self through reading this book.

Namaste.

Jeffrey Armstrong
www.JeffreyArmstrong.com

Introduction

What is necessary to change a person is to change his awareness of himself.
—ABRAHAM H. MASLOW

Many years ago, my cousin Joey came for a visit. He and my father are particularly close and have been very good to each other over the years. Every so often, Joey arranges to spend some time with my dad. On this particular occasion, the pair had gone out fishing early in the morning, and upon their return Joey approached me. Like most of my thirty cousins, he would often look at me like I had three heads. (I had chosen a very different path from the rest of my family members, and it was one they didn't quite grasp.) That day, Joey's determined expression suggested he'd gathered the courage to express something that had been on his mind. He looked at me intently and said, "You know, Gary, I've been wanting to ask you this. . . . *What exactly* is it that you do?"

I considered his question. It was a good one. I knew I had a golden opportunity here, and I didn't want to miss it. I thought for a long moment before answering.

"Well, Joey," I said, "I assist people in becoming more aware."

It was a simple, straightforward answer, and frankly, I thought it was an excellent response. I waited, and as I did, I watched Joey's expression turn from expectant to confused. He looked me right in the eye and, with total honesty, asked, "Why would anyone *want* to be more aware?"

Like many people, Joey is on a different journey; he had not yet arrived at the place in which he realized the importance of living life consciously. And that's okay, of course. At that time, he was simply not ready to embark on the journey set forth in this book: the journey that begins with awareness.

Chances are you have reached a stage in your life where you have completed many journeys and you *are* ready for the next one. You are willing to jump out of your comfort zone to take a close look at what has been holding you back from achieving that next level. Overall, you feel happy, healthy, and content, but you know that there is something more. You may find that people and things still "push your buttons," or you've come to an impasse and you're not sure why you aren't progressing, or you keep finding yourself in the same frustrating situation over and over again despite not wanting to be there. So, what's the problem? To discover this and move past the unproductive cycle of frustration and ultimately experience life in a relaxed, confident, and inspired manner, your next step is to become more aware.

By choosing this book, by reading as far as this very page, you've made yourself available for a discussion about awareness. Ultimately, you will choose whether or not you want to be aware enough to take the next step toward a greater degree of satisfaction and fulfillment in your personal and professional life. The lessons in this book will lead the way by showing you how we often fall victim to our reactions to situations and wind up becoming increasingly frustrated rather than operating from a place of balance. This will, in turn, help you to identify your personal patterns of frustration and to recognize the symptoms of your frustration as an indication that you are spinning your wheels—in other words, not making any progress toward your goals, whatever they may be. In learning this, you will also be developing important skills so that no matter where you are, no matter what's going on in your life, you will have the tools, the awareness, the practice, and the experience to be able to flow with it, whatever *it* is, with a minimum of effort and great appreciation.

We are delighted that you have given yourself the opportunity to learn how to navigate life with greater ease and well-being by breaking out of your old grooves and patterns. No matter what your role is in life—whether you are a teacher, parent, business executive, dancer, politician, artist, law-enforcement officer, student, boss, employee, child, spouse, or so on—it is important to have the necessary skills to keep you focused on the goal of greater ease in your relationships.

The exercises and practices in this book are designed to teach you how to be more fully present in your interactions with others, allowing you to experience life by *responding* (from a place of balance) rather than by *reacting* (from a place of imbalance). Having these skills helps us to operate from a more stable base and to be more involved in how our lives unfold. While there's a more analytical approach to these things, analytical examination is limited by what we already know. To go beyond, to experience the world from a more expanded state of awareness, we have to be willing to look at what is keeping us stuck in old patterns or holding us back from taking that next step, whatever it might be. Looking this closely at ourselves is something we are usually reluctant to do, but it is something we must do to grow.

As with anything, until we integrate what we learn into our experience, it is just accumulated facts, mere information. It is very easy to read a book and get useful information, but we want this book to teach you the precise steps that will enhance your experience of life. Therefore, it's not enough just to read this book. We suggest that you incorporate the skills and apply the lessons you learn here in your daily life. As you practice these steps on a regular basis, they will eventually become automatic. In our work with thousands of people over the years, Radha and I have observed that once workshop participants and clients experienced the benefits of our teachings, their confidence and ease in all types of situations increased tremendously.

RELATIONSHIPS
BEYOND PARTNERSHIP

The full meaning of the word "relationship" is often misunderstood. People tend to assume that it means a partnership, often a romantic one, between two people. While that's true in a limited sense, we are each in relationship to everything, not just other people or a significant other. Look, for instance, at a plant. Are you in relationship to that plant? You are. In fact, you and that plant have a very intimate relationship: you are nourishing each other. You are breathing in the oxygen it releases, and it is processing your exhaled carbon dioxide. Even though you know of this relationship between human beings and plant life, you probably weren't thinking past the fact that you were simply looking at the plant. As with everything, there's more to things than what you see.

Of course, something does not have to be living for you to have a relationship with it or to it. For instance, you have a relationship with the words on this page, with the book you are holding in your hands, with the chair you are sitting in, and with the sounds you are hearing. You have a relationship to concepts and ideas, places, and things. You even have a relationship with your physical body as well as with your emotions. In fact, it's all tied together; the relationship between body and mind is essential to the whole process.

There is no denying that this is a world of relationships. Relationships form the fabric of life. Through practicing the tools and experiencing the lessons in this book, you will become intimately aware of your relationship to everything, including—and most important—to yourself. And because it is this relationship to yourself that determines how you operate in the world, this is the relationship we will be examining very closely throughout these pages.

Our intention is to share this work with you so that you, too, can learn how to effortlessly and gracefully respond to agitating situations in your life. Acting from a more centered and aware place, you will intuitively know the next right thing to do for a successful or harmonic resolution or conclusion to whatever you are facing. We don't want you to try to memorize how to respond; life is too quick and the mind is too slow to be successful using that method. Rather, you are about to embark on a journey that requires regular and diligent practice so you can begin "switching off" your agitation. When you no longer allow agitation to control you, you will be more available to experience the many enlightening moments the universe has to offer.

An enlightening moment is that moment when everything makes perfect sense and the path ahead is clear. Our intuition is on full throttle. It is a moment of heightened awareness when something captures our complete, unadulterated attention, and thoughts and plans cannot interfere with our being fully present to the moment. It's a wake-up call from the universe, an awareness check. We are on a level that transcends control and manipulation, satisfaction and dissatisfaction. We are simply experiencing the moment in all of its perfection. Emotions that arise in this place are big but not overwhelming; they are beautiful but not always pleasurable. They are the moments along the journey that are unique to each and every experience when we stop and simply appreciate that which is awesome. Our feelings are heightened, and we have a powerful and precious experience—mentally, physically, and emotionally.

We've all experienced moments when we were completely balanced mentally, physically, and emotionally even in challenging situations, and we know firsthand how satisfying that feels. Yet each of us has also had experiences that seem to be just the opposite and that are very painful and disturbing where we try hard to control the situation from an imbalanced, agitated place, overanalyzing and overthinking everything. It is tedious, frustrating, confusing, and exhausting to "think" our way through life. Fortunately, flowing with events and experiencing situations as a series of enlightening moments where everything fits into place is another way, a more fulfilling way, to live life. When we live in this manner, we can face even the most challenging situations with a deep inner stability that allows us to be in perfect synchronicity with that moment.

It is our intention to help you achieve more of those moments in your daily interactions, to enjoy life with freedom, confidence, and ease. Although it took much practice, Radha and I now spend a good deal of our lives traveling from one enlightening moment to the next, like gypsies, allowing these moments to arrive naturally, simply by being available to them and noticing them when they arrive. *Everything* waits to be noticed. And that's why this journey toward greater ease in all of life's endeavors begins with awareness.

CHAPTER 1

The Journey Begins with Awareness
Shining Light on Your Path

The ultimate value of life depends upon awareness and the power of contemplation rather than upon mere survival.
—ARISTOTLE

The first step on any journey is always the most important. Without it, there is no forward movement. On this particular journey, self-reflection is essential; it is necessary for having meaningful and successful experiences in our interactions with one another, both personally and professionally. When we are unaware, we go through life enmeshed in situations, blaming people, things, and circumstances for our pain and misfortune and giving those same things credit for our joy and accomplishments. We are oblivious to what's going on inside of us and lack the freedom to step back, observe the process, and adjust. When we are unaware, we experience gaps in our consciousness, and we fill those gaps with thoughts that try to make sense of things. We determine that we are at the mercy of the waves that push us around, and we hope for calmer waters ahead. We become frustrated when the waves seem to keep throwing us off balance.

When we become aware, we can see that the waves are merely

> *Though we may not remember it, when we were toddlers we all experienced the awesome wonder of standing for the first time without falling—where suddenly a world of opportunities opened to us. Children live in the now. Their experience of life is strong and their curiosity is huge. In this process, we can be like children, looking at the world from a fresh perspective without distorting the events happening presently through the filters of our past experiences.*

obstacles in our path. We can ride them, dive below them, wait them out, jump them, or surf them. We can even calm those waves when we have the right tools at our disposal. Then, not even a powerful tsunami can throw us off course for very long.

So what is awareness? Is it something you achieve? How does it compare to thought? In this chapter, we'll take a look at these and other questions to help you take that first step on your journey toward more satisfying experiences and relationships with yourself, others, and the world around you.

THE DIFFERENCE BETWEEN AWARENESS AND THOUGHT

At its most subtle level, awareness is consciousness. It is the spark that gives us the ability to perceive and experience the world in which we reside. At its purest, that perception is unencumbered by thought and preconceived notions, and the world is therefore experienced exactly as it is: perfect in its design and intention. There are many theories on the source of that spark, but in order to embark on this journey, it isn't necessary for us to have a definitive answer to the question of its origin. Here, we simply need to accept that at the heart of the matter we are aware beings, and each of us has a certain amount of self-reflection; it can be vast, or small, or anywhere in between. Whatever the case may be, when we take steps to expand our awareness, we are giving ourselves the opportunity to experience a greater range of emotions, and this allows us to learn fully from, and grow with, the world of experiences and relationships around us. Awareness equals light. When you turn on the light, you see some of what is hidden by the darkness. When you turn up the light even brighter, you see even more. Turn up your light and see what happens.

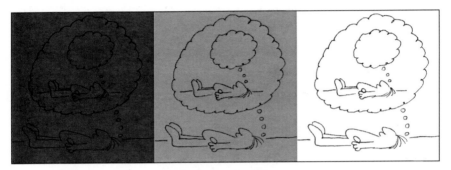

Turning up the light.

It's important to know that there are different levels of awareness. As we said previously, at its most subtle, awareness is unfettered consciousness. There are less subtle states of awareness as well. For example, we can be aware of our surroundings, other people, our body, the temperature, and so on. We can also be aware of our thoughts, beliefs, and concepts, as well as our emotions and their effect on our minds and bodies. We'll take a look at the different types of awareness in just a moment. For now, let's consider our thoughts. What are they?

Our thoughts are the labels we give to that which we perceive. I see something or I experience something, and my mind automatically labels it. I think about it. I judge it. I analyze it. I call it good. I call it bad. I connect and combine it with other thoughts. I compare it. I cherish it. I ponder it. I store it away for another time. I retrieve it from my memory banks. And so on. These labels, these thoughts, originate in the mind and are perfectly natural and useful. For example, we all know that where there's smoke, there's fire. In this case, our thoughts allow us to be aware of something we could not otherwise perceive. In this way, useful thoughts allow us to be more aware. Keep in mind, too, that thoughts aren't merely just little movies in our minds. They contain emotional content. When we think of something, we are also experiencing an emotion associated with that thought. For every single thought we have, there is a cellular response in the physical body and an emotional response in the mental body.

The mind is a wonderful tool for helping us to navigate our world, and when the mind is in harmony with the body and in its relationship to the world, we are able to glide effortlessly through our experiences with an abundance of awareness, knowing the next right step to take or thing to do (or not do). This is what we call "enlightening moments." However, what blocks us from living in that state all the time is that we are too quick to identify with our thoughts (and the emotions attached to them) and actually confuse *thinking* with *awareness*. Moreover, many of us spend inordinate amounts of time thinking about the daily drama of our lives and the secondhand drama we experience through television, movies, stories we hear from friends and family, newspapers, the Internet, books, and so on. These thoughts begin piling up in our minds, clouding our ability to clearly perceive situations and, in some cases, tainting our perception to the point of creating further unnecessary drama and turmoil. Clearly, thoughts are very powerful, and we must learn how to avoid allowing them to distort awareness. In this book and in our programs, we call thoughts "stories"; we'll discuss this in Chapter 2.

> *Thought is a function of the mind. We use our thoughts to examine and consider a situation. This is very different from bringing awareness to a situation. Thinking is an analytical process, while awareness is a direct experience; it is shining a light on something and knowing it.*

Let's return to the subject of awareness. It's important to understand this concept on an intellectual level, of course, which is why we are writing this book. But once you really absorb this information, we will help you to put it into practice in your daily life so that it becomes firsthand knowledge. Recognize and acknowledge what's going on inside you and around you, not just on an intellectual level but from a more objective state, a *knowing* place.

LEVELS OF AWARENESS

For our discussion here, it's important for you to recognize that we can be aware on three different levels: the physical level, the mental level, and the emotional level. These are different experiences of awareness, perhaps, but they are all intricately connected, so it is virtually impossible to discuss one without mentioning another. On one level, physical awareness is very rudimentary: Your body and your environment provide you with sensory data that your mind then uses to interpret your condition, and then you respond accordingly. Your foot hurts, so you sit down. There's a bear on the trail up ahead, so you back away slowly. You're hot, so you open a window. Your stomach growls, so you go in search of food. Simple enough.

Awareness of one's physical body may seem like common sense, but you'd be surprised how many people are unaware of what they are feeling on a physical level, because they don't take the time to pay attention, to apply awareness to it. (The light of awareness is too dim, so they cannot "feel" it.) Some people cannot identify when a muscle is being engaged or do not realize that they are tensing up in an uncomfortable situation. Other people end up overeating because they aren't paying attention to the signals from their stomach. It's important to be aware of the body's physical sensations and signals. Start to increase your physical awareness by putting your attention on various parts of your body and focusing on the subtle sensations. For example, while you are reading this, feel your body. Do you have any aches or pains? Are you sitting in a comfortable position? Are you thirsty? Do you need to get up and stretch? Throughout the day, consciously place attention on your body to become more attune to what it is telling you.

As mentioned earlier, every thought we have is connected to an emotion with varying degrees of intensity. Because an emotion is a dynamic relationship between the mind and body, every thought we think has a direct effect on our bodies, some more noticeable than others. The moment-to-moment changes that take place in our bodies can reveal a tremendous amount of information if we know how to "feel for them." Every single thought we have, no matter what it might be, as well as every emotion we experience, is immediately received by corresponding cells in our brain and amplified and transmitted throughout our bodies. Therefore, when we think something, our body feels it. It becomes a physical sensation. It's very important to recognize that every single emotion and thought in our mind is immediately experienced and recorded and sometimes stored in our physical body. For example, after an emotional encounter you may have a pain in your neck, or before an important event you may have "butterflies" in your stomach, or upon seeing a newborn child you may literally feel lighter.

If you know how to look for them, these physical sensations can be fairly obvious. If you have not been trained to recognize these emotions, the next time you get upset, observe which part of your

DEALING WITH OUR EMOTIONS

We teach that there are two ways people deal with emotions: response or reaction. When we respond, we are doing so from a state of balance in which we accept the emotions we are feeling and behave in an appropriate manner. A response is always fresh and new. When we react, however, we are doing so from a place of imbalance. We reject the emotions we are feeling and behave reflexively without examining those feelings, in such a way as to get rid of, or reject, them. A reaction is generally based on some past experience or preconceived notion. While the preferred method is to respond, reactions offer a tremendous amount of information about what is happening to us subconsciously. They are portals that allow us to look inside and create the clear transformation we are heading toward.

body is affected (shallow breath? tight shoulders? jumpy stomach?). When you become more aware of the effect that thoughts and their accompanying emotions have on your physical being, you'll begin to notice even subtler changes in your body, which are important clues to what is going on at the subconscious levels of your behavior.

Try to become aware also of your mental processes, your thoughts. To increase your mental awareness, observe yourself thinking. Take note of your thoughts and the emotional content of those thoughts. Hear the messages you are telling yourself. If you develop the habit of observing yourself think, you will be in a better position to recognize the messages when your subconscious programming (what's going on beneath your consciousness) begins to come to the surface through your work in this book.

Research shows that 99 percent of mental functioning occurs beneath the surface at the subconscious level. Being aware of this can spur us onward in our journey to shed more light on how we operate. To really be able to know ourself and change, it is

necessary to be aware of this hidden operating system. We need to bring these subconscious thoughts and emotions to the surface—in other words, we need to increase our mental and emotional awareness. Some emotions are simply felt and then pass away in the ordinary course of a moment, hour, day, or week. However, other emotions are experienced like explosions and can be so overwhelming that we do not know what to do with them. In our discomfort, we react without knowing why and attempt to escape from the discomfort through our "preferred method" of distraction or through a compulsive reaction. A good first step in stopping yourself from distracting is being able to identify the emotion you are feeling. See "Identifying Emotions" on the next page.

IDENTIFYING EMOTIONS

We are all familiar with the "big" emotions—love, fear, joy, and anger—but the full spectrum of emotions is much more varied. Since most of us haven't had formal training to recognize exactly what we're feeling, there may be certain emotions that we can't identify even though we are feeling them. Take a look at the list below and explore how these various emotions might feel to you, and think of a situation in which you may have felt that emotion. Throughout the day, be curious about what you are feeling. Refer back to this list as often as you need to.

Acceptance	Cheer	Discovery
Adequacy	Closeness	Disgust
Agony	Comfort	Disrespect
Amusement	Compassion	Distance
Anger	Competitiveness	Doubtfulness
Annoyance	Completion	Eagerness
Anticipation	Composure	Elation
Anxiety	Concern	Embarrassment
Apathy	Confidence	Empathy
Appreciation	Confusion	Energy
Apprehensiveness	Contempt	Enmity
Assuredness	Courage	Enthusiasm
Awe	Cowardice	Envy
Boldness	Cruelty	Exasperation
Boredom	Delight	Excellence
Burdened	Depression	Excitement
Calmness	Destructiveness	Exhaustion
Capability	Detachment	Exhilaration
Caution	Determination	Expectation
Certainty	Disappointment	Familiarity
Charm	Discomfort	Fascination

Fear	Joy	Respect
Fearlessness	Jumpiness	Revenge
Friendship	Kindness	Sadness
Frustration	Loneliness	Satisfaction
Gladness	Loss	Secure
Glamour	Love	Serenity
Glee	Lust	Shame
Glory	Magnificence	Shamelessness
Goodness	Manipulation	Shock
Gracefulness	Misery	Sorrow
Greatness	Modesty	Stability
Greed	Nervousness	Strength
Grief	Pain	Stress
Guilt	Panic	Sublimity
Happiness	Patience	Superiority
Hate	Peaceful	Surprise
Hesitancy	Pity	Suspicion
Hope	Playfulness	Sympathy
Hostility	Pleasantness	Terror
Humor	Pleasure	Thrill
Ignored	Positivity	Timidity
Impatience	Possessiveness	Tiredness
Incompleteness	Pressure	Togetherness
Indifference	Pride	Tolerance
Indignation	Privacy	Uneasiness
Innocence	Rage	Unhappiness
Inspiration	Rashness	Unkindness
Interest	Rejection	Wariness
Intimidation	Relaxation	Wasteful
Irritation	Relief	Weariness
Isolation	Remorse	Wonder
Jealousy	Repentance	

SHINING LIGHT ON THE VIRUS
IN THE OPERATING SYSTEM

Let's shift our awareness for a moment and consider that our bodies are the hardware of a sophisticated computer that runs all of our systems via the senses, and our mind contains the operating system that runs that computer. Our experiences from birth onward program the software that determines how the operating system functions through the hardware—that is, how we perceive and act in the world. Now consider the source of these experiences: parents, siblings, other family members, teachers, playmates, celebrities, politicians, large purple alien creatures, and so on. All of these people are the programmers of our software. It is not too much of a stretch to consider that with so many programmers some faulty information, or viruses, will end up infecting our program. By the time we become adults, this operating software is so much a part of our makeup that we might not even be aware that our software is full of bugs.

When we become aware through this work of self-reflection that there is a virus in our operating system, we can then learn how to deactivate it. Keep in mind that it's not a matter of *whether* the program is faulty; we all have faulty (less than healthy) programming to some degree. If we are aware enough and brave enough to admit it, we can all identify with one or more erroneous core beliefs (something we believe about our nature that is absolutely untrue), such as *I'm not good enough,* or *I'm not safe,* or *I'm all alone,* or countless variations of such statements. These *erroneous core beliefs* are the viruses in our operating system. As you continue on this journey and apply what you learn in this book, you will discover which "virus" is being activated and how it throws you off balance. With this better understanding and a closer look at what's going on within you, you will discover how to deactivate unhealthy programs whenever they threaten to run your operating system. (Erroneous core beliefs are discussed in Chapter 3.)

UNDERSTANDING THAT WE ARE *NOT* OUR MINDS

There is very little discussion in our society about what the mind really is. One dictionary definition is "the seat of thought and memory, thinking capacity, concentration, and way of thinking." But these are only functions of the mind (thinking, memory, concentration), so this doesn't really give us a clear understanding of what the mind is. This definition is analogous to answering, "What is a human being?" by describing our digestive system. Functionality is revealing, of course, but only when we know what something is in the first place.

It is important for us to know that the mind is a vehicle with a very specific function. It enables us to sense the world. It gives us an identity and allows us to experience ourselves in relationship to the things and events around us. Because we have a mind, we are able to perceive the material world, remember what we have experienced, and make conclusions based on what we believe is true. (If I do not identify myself as a man, I might mistakenly walk into the ladies' room.) The mind records events and keeps us in continuity with our life. When it is working properly, we remember our name and where we live. The mind is a rather useful vehicle; however, just as a car needs a driver to steer it, our mind also needs an operator. In other words, it needs us to operate *it,* not the other way around. Awareness is supposed to drive the mind.

In our culture, we have little information or guidance that lets us know that we *have* a mind, although we are *not* the mind. Try this experiment: Stare at your right hand and focus on your fingers and nails; look at their shape and size. Then, after a minute, ask yourself, *Am I this hand?* Of course, your reply will be an emphatic, *No! I am the one who is observing my hand, so how could I be my hand? Besides, this hand has changed so many times during the course of my life that I could not possibly be something that is constantly changing over time. I am the one thing in my life that does not change. I am the observer of my hand, my foot, my torso, and so on, but I am not my body.*

Continuing with this line of thought, close your eyes and recite the alphabet. Did you witness yourself reciting the alphabet? If not, do it again. This time, while you are reciting the alphabet, observe your mind performing the task. Notice that you can actually observe your mind reciting the alphabet. Now, recall what you ate for breakfast, lunch, and dinner yesterday. Observe your mind as it retrieves the information, remembering the details of your meals. The same way  you observed your hand, you are observing your mind as it processes information. If you can observe your mind, then you cannot be the mind. Do you see how simple this is? If I am observing a sunset . . . well, you get the point. Now ask yourself whether or not your mind stays in one place (remains static) or if it's in constant movement. Become familiar with how your mind works. This is the first step in learning how to make your mind work for you.

It is true that it's possible to train our minds to remain completely undisturbed by thoughts, and when this occurs we experience clarity and insight (which is what we call an enlightening moment). In this state, solutions come to us more readily. For now, it's important to know that it is possible to observe your mind as your thoughts are being created. When looked at this way, it is easy to accept the theory that we are more than the contents of our ever-changing mind, that we are the observers of our thoughts, and further that we are the observers of our emotions, and as we recall events, we are the observers of our memories. As the observer, we function as the source of awareness, and since this journey begins with awareness, the more often we watch our thoughts, emotions, and physical sensations, the more awareness becomes available in our lives.

Throughout the course of the day, when we observe the many situations unfolding before us, we will be in a better position to notice all the subtleties. Thus, our ability to read between the lines and our intuition become greatly enhanced. In fact, this isn't entirely new. We have been observing ourselves throughout our lives; it's just a process of enhancing this awareness. For example, I have a memory of being in a hospital and looking through the bars of my crib at a row of toy trucks and cars on the floor. My mother confirmed that I was in such a room when I was two years old for a hernia operation. And, yes, as the story goes, I had all my toys with me for the two-day hospital stay. Who is it that is observing a memory from more than sixty years ago? That part of me that remembers that scene, looking through the bars of a crib when I was two years old, is an aware being who has the ability to use my mind and body, instead of being used by my mind and body, to navigate this material world successfully.

Now that we are aware that we have the capacity to observe our mind, we can notice our thoughts and emotions more objectively. This new perspective gives us an edge over people who believe that they are their minds. Being the observer of the mind gives us the advantage of remaining objective in difficult situations, which results in decisions that are not influenced by anything but clarity, intuition, and unbiased knowing.

Contemplate the fact that you are not your mind until you truly believe that you possess the skill to observe your thoughts and emotions without becoming lost in them (the awareness exercises throughout the book will help you do this). You are an aware being with a physical body, a mind, and many emotions. The more awareness you have in your life, the less likely you will be tricked into believing that the big, upsetting emotion you just experienced is you. When you know they are not you, you can deal with upsetting emotions in a more aware, more objective fashion. This will result in less frustration, pain, and suffering. Of course, the reverse is equally true; when you operate with less awareness, there will be more frustration, pain, and suffering. As you continue through these teachings, you will learn how to end what we call the Frustration Cycle, by operating from the place of observer—that part of you that is in control of your mind.

BRINGING YOUR HABITS, TENDENCIES, AND PATTERNS TO THE FOREFRONT

Being fully aware of and recognizing your habits and tendencies—in other words, shedding more light on your patterns—is essential to the process outlined in this book and in our programs. It's important that you begin placing your awareness not only on your thoughts, your body, and your surroundings, as we've discussed, but *especially* on your reactions to circumstances and the activities you engage in. When we become aware that we have consistent reactions to certain situations or that we are engaging in some repetitive behavior, we are in the position to ask, *Why am I reacting? What's going on? Why am I doing this?* We don't want to disregard that reaction and/or distract from it since we're bound to face the same or similar situations again (that's the frustrating thing about life: we keep facing the same upsetting situations without seeing any changes take place). Nor do we want to blindly continue to engage in useless behavior without being aware of why we are doing it. This is where the ability to breathe deeply, relax, and not jump to conclusions comes in handy! Without techniques, we are still bound to our old reflexive patterns.

 To begin responding to situations rather than reacting to them, you need to envision pressing a "pause button." If you feel yourself reacting to a situation in which you're not sure what's going on, take a step back. Why continue down the same old path? This is your opportunity to try an alternate route. Pausing allows you to calm your mind, refocus your attention, and come back into balance. By taking a moment (or longer) and considering what's at play and using your discrimination, you are actively increasing your awareness of both yourself and the circumstances. While your pause button is activated, try to determine where the stress is located in your body; whether you are breathing correctly; if you feel out of balance, rigid, or weak; whether you want to fight or run away; and whether or not you feel victimized. For now, simply notice all this and be aware of these many thoughts and emotions.

Another way to look at the pause button is as an intermission of sorts. This is an enjoyable awareness-enhancing exercise. Try thinking of yourself as an actor in a play. As children, we all played at being something else, so this is relatively easy to do. But now, also try to think of yourself as a member of an audience, so that you are both in the play *and* watching it. Observe the situations around you and see how you move through them. Pay careful attention to the other actors

THE GROOVES IN THE MIND

Each time we have an experience, our brain records it, creating a physical pathway from neuron to neuron. The next time we have a similar experience, the mind will take us along that same pathway. The more often we have that experience, the more trodden that pathway becomes. When we engage in something time and time again, the mind starts to become accustomed to taking that particular, well-worn path. Then, any deviation from that pathway starts to feel uncomfortable or unnatural. Suddenly we are faced with deep grooves in the mind and our thoughts and reactions become ingrained and automatic, seemingly almost out of our control, as if we are operating in a trance or sleepwalking. We become stuck in concepts or preconceived notions. This is how habits and patterns form. If these experiences are negative or unfulfilling, the pathways formed serve us no purpose. They decrease our awareness because we are not looking outside our patterned reaction for a more suitable response. In Chapter 4, we'll look more closely at our patterns in an effort to unravel them and form more productive pathways.

and the lines your character delivers in response to their lines. As is often the case, the production is proceeding nicely, all of the characters are playing their parts, everything is going smoothly . . . then bam! The drama begins. It's a situation your character has encountered before. Your immediate reaction is to shout, withdraw, deliver a biting comment, or any number of *reactive* responses. But when you pause before responding, you do nothing. Why? Because it's intermission. The curtains close. You take a break. This break, this pause, gives you a chance to consider the next scene, what lines your character is going to deliver, and the manner in which those lines will be delivered. As the observer, this gives you a chance to go outside, get some fresh air, and perhaps have some refreshment. If your desired outcome is to be in harmony, now you have a chance to use your discrimination to determine how that harmony can best be achieved by what happens next. You have the opportunity to rewrite your script.

This pause in the action is a good time to engage in a relaxation technique. Practice this when you have the time:

Sit back in a comfortable chair or lie down on your back with your legs bent, supported by a pillow if you desire. Start by taking a few deep breaths through your nose, extending the exhalation slowly and easefully. Once you are comfortable, begin to direct each breath into another part of your body. Start by directing your attention to your feet, ankles, calves, then thighs. As you inhale, visualize that the breath reaches into the physical area on which you are focusing. As you exhale, visualize that the tension in that area releases.

Now place your attention on your fingers and hands . . . forearms . . . upper arms. Next, place your attention on your pelvis . . . buttocks . . . abdomen . . . chest . . . lower back . . . middle back . . . shoulder blades. Make sure that you are breathing slowly, not rushing, and allow yourself to really feel the body parts with your mind and awareness.

Finally, focus your attention on your neck . . . throat . . . jaw . . . lips. Relax your tongue, cheeks, nose, eyes, and forehead. With your physical body relaxed, you can now allow your breath to go back to its natural rhythm. Attempt to just observe the movement of the breath flowing into the body and then out. You should notice a deep state of stillness and relaxation at this point.

There is nothing to do except enjoy the experience. At some point you will be ready to go back to your daily activities, feeling refreshed and clearer. You can also use this technique at bedtime if you have trouble sleeping or when you wake up in the middle of the night and can't get back to sleep.

This relaxation technique works well if the situation doesn't require an immediate response, like if you receive an upsetting text message or e-mail and you do not need to respond right away. However, if you must respond right away, mastering your breath is essential. Often, when we are in a stressful situation, our breathing becomes shallow or labored or we hold our breath. Becoming aware of your breath when you become agitated and being able to control it is an on-the-spot pause button. Do the Breathing for Awareness Exercise on page 30 and practice it often so that you can use it whenever necessary. As the breath deepens, the mind begins to experience more clarity.

> *The breath is an essential component for keeping the mind clear and allowing us to deal with the upsets in our life.*

ESSENTIAL SKILLS FOR THE JOURNEY

To truly embark on this journey and successfully navigate through challenging times, we need three essential skills:

- ◆ Balance
- ◆ Strength
- ◆ Flexibility

If we are coming from an unbalanced, rigid, weak place, our interactions with the world will reflect that, and so our practice is to nurture these qualities in ourselves so that they are reflected back to us in our relationships. When we possess these skills, we can change direction very quickly. When faced with the winding, rocky, and uncertain path that life sets before us, having these skills can keep us out of harm's way and help us travel almost effortlessly with the changing terrain. There are fewer obstacles in our path because there is less interference from outside influences. Therefore, it's essential to develop these skills. That's why in this area, it's all about practice. Begin now to focus on developing these qualities on three levels: the mental, the emotional, and the physical. Adopt those practices, many of which are described in the following sections, that will allow you to increase these qualities. When we possess them in all areas of our life, we have more clarity, and more awareness is therefore available to us.

The Importance of Proper Nutrition

Since our physical body is the base from which we operate, it's very important to keep our cells nourished with a proper diet. Paying close attention to the foods we eat and becoming aware of what we put into our body are essential steps in the process. This is because every cell in the body affects, and is affected by, the thoughts and emotions present in the mind. As the familiar maxim states, "You are what you eat." So, taking notice of how different foods affect us gives us a glimpse into the connection between our diet and the mind. For example, how many times have you felt lazy after a big holiday meal? How often do you depend on that first cup of morning coffee to get your brain started? The connection between our diet and how it affects our mental state is obvious if we take the time to notice it. Begin now to really get in touch with how what you eat affects not only your body but also your thinking. Does it slow it down or speed it up? Does it increase your thoughts or help clear your mind?

The reason food has a direct impact on our mental and emotional states is because whatever is happening in our physical body is simultaneously experienced in our mind. If we are emotionally upset, many of us find ourselves with pains, such as a backache, stiff neck, upset stomach, or headache. This is because of the direct relationship between the mind and the body. The reverse is also true. When we consume agitating foods, they eventually create agitation in the mind; we cannot separate the two. For example, if you have a cup of chamomile tea at night, it not only relaxes your body but soothes your mind as well, preparing it for sleep. Compare this to eating a pepperoni pizza sprinkled with hot peppers and washing it down with a large glass of cola right before bed. You can expect to experience a restless night's sleep—if you sleep at all!

There are three basic categories of food: those that make us sluggish (such as cheese and other animal products, overripe fruits, alcohol, and heavily processed foods), those that agitate us (such as garlic, onions, caffeine, refined sugar, and pungent spices), and those that are balanced (such as fresh fruits, vegetables, and whole grains). In the same way, there are also three categories of thoughts and emotions: sluggish ones (such as laziness and boredom), agitating ones (such as desire, anger, resentment, and jealousy), and balanced ones (such as love, compassion, peacefulness, and empathy). As you have probably guessed by now, developing men-

tal awareness depends on cultivating balanced thoughts and providing our bodies with balanced foods. Since being more aware enhances every aspect of life, it serves us well to eat foods that will increase the amount of awareness we bring to our daily lives.

The Importance of a Healthy Body

Besides the food we eat, the overall health of our bodies is also dependent on the activities we engage in regularly. Just like an automobile, our bodies require more than just fuel. If you take your car in for a tune-up, the mechanic will check the tire pressure, lubricate the moving parts, and make sure it is functioning at its highest possible level. Not every car is the same, however. We would never expect a VW Beetle to go as fast as a Lamborghini. There are different models of automobiles, each having specific features and maintenance requirements. Similarly, there are different bodies, each having specific advantages and challenges. Overall, our bodies need to be strong, flexible, and balanced to perform at their optimum level. For this reason, proper exercise is essential to maintaining a healthy body. To increase your physical balance, strength, and flexibility, it's important to engage in a regular exercise routine that allows you to develop these skills, such as biking, swimming, brisk walking, and other non-impact routines. Yoga, especially hatha yoga, is known for developing a strong, flexible, balanced body, as well as a strong, focused, and concentrated mind. If you don't already have a regular exercise routine, now is a good time to start participating in physical activities you enjoy.

When our minds are balanced and clear, flexible to new ideas, and strong enough to remain focused, we are more successful in navigating challenging situations. The healthier the body and mind, the less physical and mental agitation, and thus the more awareness will be present. While all successful athletes have healthy bodies, there are many examples of professional athletes who have gotten into trouble in their personal lives. This is an indicator that while the body is balanced, flexible, and strong, the same is not necessarily true for the mind. On the other end of the spectrum, there are many talented people—intellectually, artistically, or financially—who suffer a decrease in awareness because they have imbalances in their physical bodies. A person who has a healthy body* *and* mind will have more awareness available than a person who possesses only one or the other. This is why it's important to focus on maintaining both a healthy mind and body to be successful with this program.

The Importance of Mental Focus

The ability to focus the mind is an essential ingredient in this work. Without being able to clear the mind of distracting thoughts, we are like a boat on the ocean of life without a rudder, oar, sail, or motor drifting aimlessly among the waves of thoughts that pass in front of us daily. Many scientific studies have concluded that a regular meditation practice increases the strength of the immune system, keeps us in balance during agitating events, and allows us to remain flexible to new ideas. The ability to clear the mind of random thoughts allows us to be more available to the invitations that life

> *A strong, flexible, and balanced mind and body results in being more present to your life.*

offers. For example, if you are lost in thought while driving along a country road, you might miss your turn or you might not see the delightful fruit stand waiting for you to pull over and enjoy a delicious apple. Without focus, that invitation would be missed. A clear mind allows us to remain more relaxed without relying on old, familiar patterns that have defined our personality and often limit us from engaging in the new and exciting possibilities ahead.

When we practice meditation, we become more mentally flexible and able to accept life's challenges rather than being overwhelmed by them or trying to control them. Mental strength is improved because the mind is no longer distracted. A focused, undistracted mind is able to remain steadfast and strong rather than getting caught up in "noise" (distracting thoughts). In a state of meditation, there are no upsets.

---

*This is not to say that people with physical challenges cannot experience increased awareness, of course. A healthy body is a body that is as healthy as can be under its present circumstances.

Since the state of meditation is a state of ease, the brain and nervous system is rejuvenated by the practice. Meditation can be practiced while we're active, or an even deeper state can be achieved when we disengage from the outside world by closing our eyes, breathing deeply, and allowing our attention to rest upon pure awareness.

Most people who meditate regularly experience less stress, have fewer health problems, perform at a higher level, and can better deal with challenging situations without losing balance. From this place of serenity, they remain flexible and steadfast during all their interactions.

The Importance of Dealing with Your Emotions

Aside from balance, strength, and flexibility on the physical and mental levels, these qualities are essential on the emotional level as well since our emotions directly affect our physical and mental states. If we are emotionally unbalanced, we may do things to make ourselves feel better temporarily, such as overeating, surfing the Internet, or turning on the television to "zone out" at the end of a mentally taxing day. While "solutions" such as these may work in the short term, they actually provide little more than distractions that lead to unhealthy patterns. There are so many distractions available to us that in order to be successful in life, we need to be as aware as possible. (Chapters 3 and 4 will help you in this regard.)

A person who is in excellent physical, mental, and emotional shape has an advantage over those whose awareness is limited by dis-ease and its precursor, imbalance. For example, if someone is experiencing bodily discomfort, mental agitation, or emotional distress, it is easy to see how this could easily lead to poor choices on many different levels. The more we remain in a balanced, strong, and flexible state on these three levels—physical, mental, and emotional—the more awareness we have available to make smart choices, good decisions, and strengthen our relationship with ourselves and the world around us.

Liz's Experience
BECOMING AWARE OF HER BREATH

Liz was stuck in the deep groove of a smoker's reaction to stress. Whenever she felt uncomfortable, she would reach for a cigarette. This was a patterned reaction she had developed over many years. Despite being healthy in other ways, she was stuck in the inflexible thought that she could only deal with stress in this destructive manner. She actually believed that cigarettes relaxed her, while in reality, the nicotine was triggering an adrenal reaction that was physically agitating her body. Because of this habit, her system was out of balance and her strength was compromised. Her physical, mental, and emotional levels were not in harmony. By shining a light on her patterned responses, it slowly dawned on her that smoking was her automatic response to agitating thoughts. Once she realized that she possessed the strength to challenge those thoughts head-on, she was able to successfully quit smoking.

Once she was free of this distraction and was slowly regaining her equilibrium, she discovered that it wasn't so much the thoughts but the emotions attached to them that were the source of her discomfort. What she realized was that emotions—especially the uncomfortable ones—are quite powerful and often difficult to navigate. Her awareness had increased just enough to keep her from wanting to turn to her old standby, but without that crutch she had arrived at a very unsettled, unbalanced place in her life.

Liz learned early on in the program that achieving balance begins with the breath. But first, she had to become *aware* of her breath. Ironically, she'd been breathing in smoke for so long as her way of coping that she didn't realize that she could have simply breathed in fresh air. Her first tool in successfully navigating the world of emotions and relationships on the journey toward experiencing more of life's wonderful offerings was the Breathing for Awareness Exercise.

❧ Breathing for Awareness Exercise ❧

In this book and in our programs, we specifically target whatever prevents us from being fully aware in the moments available to us. We don't just want to know this intellectually; we want to know it in our bodies. So, the first exercise is about becoming more aware of what is going on inside of us. Our breath is the first clue. We have a very intimate relationship with the way we breathe in and the way we breathe out, but very few people are aware of it. This exercise guides you through the process of knowing more about your breathing, and, therefore, more about what's happening in your body on a very deep level.

In our society, we are told to keep our abdomen tight, but it is important that the abdomen is relaxed when we breathe to allow the diaphragm to release and allow the lungs to take in more air. So, for this exercise, we want you to use the Three-Part Breath. First, you breathe into your abdomen, which expands your rib cage; then you fill up your lungs. Think of it like filling a glass with water. The water goes to the bottom of the glass first. Likewise, your breath goes into your abdomen first. This expands your rib cage (the middle of the glass). Then fill your upper lungs (the top of the glass). Then, conversely, when you exhale, pour the water out of the glass from the top, the middle, and the bottom. Think of that image when you are breathing out.

Now, take a gentle breath in through your nose, keeping your lips closed and your teeth apart. Inhale deeply. Pause for a moment and then exhale very slowly, also through your nose. As you exhale, count how many seconds pass until all of the air is out of your lungs. Do this several times, breathing in and out for one minute and continue to count the seconds as you exhale. At the end of the minute, average out the length of your exhalations and round it down to an even number. That is your exhalation count. The target is to create a 1:2 ratio. In other words, your inhalation should be half the count of your exhalation. So if you exhale for 6 seconds, your inhalation will be 3. The average count is 5 seconds on the inhalation and 10 on the exhalation. Anything less than that suggests that your body is in a state of tension because you are not getting enough oxygen. (Always seek the advice of a healthcare practitioner if you have shortness of breath or any other breathing difficulties.) The ideal count is 10 in and 20 out, but don't expect to reach that goal right away. Take it in small steps by practicing this technique often.

Record your inhalation/exhalation count and date it. Each time your count increases, record and date it. Ideally, practice this exercise three times a day for at least five minutes at a time. This allows your brain to begin to recognize the changes in the carbon dioxide and oxygen levels in your bloodstream. It will take a minimum of six weeks for your body to become used to this new balance and accept it as its normal state.

It's very important to understand that when a person becomes stressed, his or her breathing generally becomes shallower, thereby increasing carbon dioxide in the blood. Is there a chicken-and-egg sort of relationship here? Can you train your breath so that your body is more relaxed, creating a calmer mental state? The answer is a resounding *yes*. Practice this exercise often so that when a challenge does occur, you are prepared because you have better control of your breath and the more relaxed mental state that accompanies it.

JOURNALING

Throughout this book and, more important, on this journey of increasing awareness, you will be engaging in what we call "Experiences for the Road." These experiential activities give you the chance to apply what you've learned in each chapter out in the world—through your interactions with people, in nature, and with yourself. You will want to invest in a journal to take notes when prompted or whenever you feel compelled to share with yourself what you've discovered. This is a good place to note your breath count from the Breathing for Awareness Exercise and update it from time to time.

Journaling is one of the easiest and most effective ways to learn about ourselves. It allows us to place our thoughts and emotions on paper where we can examine them as we record them and later as we reflect upon them. Through journaling, we can discover what we believe, why we believe it, and, most important, how we feel about it. Many of us are unaware of what truly motivates us. Regular journaling provides us with an opportunity to recognize how certain patterns seem to pop up time and again over the course of our lives. Journaling helps to integrate intellectual and emotional awareness or, to put it another way, to connect the head to the heart.

Here's a good analogy: if your exercise program targets a certain muscle group, the result is that the targeted group is strengthened. For example, in a hatha yoga class, if you are practicing a one-legged balancing pose, such as the tree pose, your leg muscles, abdominals, and brain are stimulated and strengthened, and the benefits remain long after the class. In the same manner, whenever you focus your attention on some part of your self, the awareness of that part automatically increases. Journaling enhances your mental and emotional awareness, not just while you are recording your thoughts, but long after you've performed the journaling exercise.

❧ *Experience for the Road* ❧

For this first Experience for the Road activity, make a concerted effort to be more aware of your physical reality, your mental reality, and your emotional reality. Take time to really observe yourself while you're out in the world going about your daily activities—working, parenting, socializing, and so on—and begin to take note of your reactions. Be aware of what's going on, not just mentally but also what's going on in your body. For example, when you get upset, you might notice that your breathing becomes shallow, or you experience tightness in your chest. Take note of this. Become aware that what's happening on the mental or emotional level is affecting the physical level. We can't be well versed in how our bodies react on the physical level if we don't focus our awareness on it. Of course, you know in your head when you are upset about something because you are constantly churning it around in there and watching all those thoughts go by. But now make an effort to also be aware of what's happening on the physical level.

As you become upset or agitated during the course of a day, make a mental note or write in your journal the upsetting circumstance, the emotion that you are experiencing, and where it is manifesting in your body. Really pay attention to this. The more awareness you give it, the more you will be able to recognize it without trying. Likewise, if you feel uneasiness in your body, try to identify the associated emotion and the circumstance that may have triggered it. This information will be very useful to you in the following chapters.

The intention of this chapter was to clarify the difference between awareness and thought, and to offer some insight on how to increase your awareness on different levels. The biggest takeaway we hope you got from this chapter is that you have the ability to experience life through this awareness rather than through old programmed thoughts and emotions, and that you can achieve clarity and move through life with greater ease.

So, if we have the ability to clear our minds, expand our awareness, and experience life as a series of enlightening moments, why
don't we just go ahead and do that? Why can't we just turn a switch
and be in those special moments at will? Why don't we live in that
perfect place all of the time no matter what's going on in our lives?
What's the problem? What's stopping us? In the next chapter, we'll
take a step closer to learning what it is.

CHAPTER 2

What Is It?
Identifying the Situation and the Story

*There is nothing either good or bad,
but thinking makes it so.*

—WILLIAM SHAKESPEARE

What upsets or frustrates you? When you become agitated, do you know *which* of your buttons are getting pushed? Do you know *when* they get pushed? Do you know *how* they get pushed? Are you even aware that your buttons are being pushed? You might not be. You might be blaming your frustration on something outside yourself. Have you noticed that sometimes you get upset about something that at other times doesn't bother you? This is similar to two people reacting differently to the same situation. For instance, have you listened to someone's story of an upsetting event and thought, *I wonder why she got so upset by that?* (You may even look back on your own reaction to some recent event and wonder why you overreacted.)

To begin to unravel what's going on, in this chapter we are going to look at two important factors: the situation and the story. Understanding these factors and their roles will help you begin to identify the cause of your agitation or discomfort. This is the first step in dealing directly with your frustration, and it is just the beginning of the process of exiting the Frustration Cycle (which we'll discuss in Chapter 4). For now, let's take a look at these two factors.

EXAMINING THE SITUATION

Situations are the events that are happening around us. They make up our everyday experiences; some may be opportunities for growth, while others may not have any obvious effect on us. In other words, we'll just feel neutral about the circumstances surrounding an event. In other cases, we'll feel a certain amount of satisfaction, and yet in other instances, we'll feel some level of agitation that can easily mutate into frustration. It isn't the situation—the outside influence—that is really the source of our agitated feelings. There's much more to it. The outcome we hope to achieve is that when we see the situation from a new perspective, what previously "drove us to distraction" won't have the same impact. Learning how to do this takes deep understanding and a lot of practice.

It is easy to mistake our story (our running narrative *about* an event) for the situation, and when this happens, quite a bit of confusion develops, which can perpetuate the agitation. So to avoid this, let's learn how to discern the difference between outward situations and our story. A situation can contain any number of variables, but it is *always* based on fact. Here are some examples of situations:

◆ Sixty-year-old George is the president of the board of directors for a tremendously successful business on the stock exchange, who has difficulty setting boundaries with people in his personal life.

◆ Thirty-year-old Jason, a student, teacher, and writer, is dating a woman who he loves but who does not love him in return, although she does not want to end the relationship.

◆ Twenty-five-year-old Carolina, an accountant, recently divorced her husband, who behaved in a verbally abusive manner throughout much of their marriage.

◆ Fifty-year-old Michael, a head research scientist who established and runs a research facility, lost his fourth qualified employee in the same number of years and needs to find a replacement.

◆ Thirty-eight-year-old Cynthia, a successful entrepreneur, has been divorced twice and wants to get married and have children.

◆ Forty-two-year-old Mark is a lieutenant colonel in the U.S. Army whose assignment is to assist families of soldiers killed in action. He is twice divorced and lives part-time with his two daughters.

◆ Fifty-three-year-old William has high blood pressure for which he must take medication.

◆ Fifty-six-year-old Stephanie, a successful bodyworker, has a pile of unopened mail, unpaid bills, and unanswered e-mails to attend to.

◆ Forty-year-old Keith, a self-employed executive headhunter, spends hours online surfing the Web and making occasional purchases.

◆ Thirty-one-year-old Veronica, a yoga instructor, is at odds with her business partner over how to run the business.

◆ Forty-seven-year-old Bethany, a manager of a health-food store, experiences discomfort around the owner of the store, who the employees agree behaves aggressively.

Notice that none of these situations contain subjective information. Without subjectivity, these situations cannot be labeled as good or bad, negative or positive. In other words, when we are looking at just the situation, a cigar will *always* be just a cigar. It is only when we bring ourselves and all of our accumulated experiences that shape our perception into the equation that we begin to size up the circumstances surrounding an event and make conclusions about it.

Let's take a look at Keith's situation: he spends hours online. Is that a problem? Well, spending time online is not a problem in and of itself. For example, a research assistant might spend hours online in order to accomplish his or her research goals, or a student might spend hours online in group study, and so on. Keith, however, was not accomplishing anything worthwhile in his own estimation. In other words, Keith might say, "I'm wasting all my time on the Internet." And, for Keith, that statement brings up all sorts of feelings and other statements, such as "I'm such a slacker for not getting my work done," in a domino-like effect. Do you see how the situation *seemed* to change when Keith's perspective was introduced? In actuality, the situation didn't change at all. Subjective information was introduced along with another situation: Keith wasn't getting his work done. It was a simple fact. Calling himself a slacker, however, was an opinion he had of himself and not part of the situation. So, in other words, the situation wasn't responsible for Keith's poor opinion of himself, but rather Keith was. Let's take a look at Cynthia's situation, too. She would like to get married and start a family. That's a basic human desire. However, she is pressuring herself to get it done and get on with it before her biological clock runs out. She is worrying that there won't be enough time and that she'll never have the love she is longing for from a husband and child. Cynthia is focused on the future, and to her it looks dismal.

Situations can be short-term events too, like standing in line at the grocery store, as well as long-term events like those described above, such as searching for a spouse. Let's say there are three women waiting in line at a grocery store. The cashier suddenly abandons her station, saying she'll be back in a moment (she needed to take an emergency bathroom break, but did not communicate that to the women). That's the situation: *the cashier suddenly abandons her station.* Each woman will likely experience the situation differently. One has to get home to meet the school bus and is therefore worried she won't make it on time but realizes the cashier must have had a good reason to leave her station and the break was not a personal attack. The second has no appointments pending but still experiences some mild annoyance that the cashier would just "abandon her," and then she distracts herself with a tabloid and a candy bar. The third (who also has no appointments pending) becomes agitated, angry that the cashier had the nerve to waste her time, and starts huffing and puffing.

Do you see how the same exact situation resulted in three different perceptions?

Here's another example. The CEO of a corporation presents the financials at a scheduled meeting. In reviewing the documents, one executive's heart starts pounding because he thinks the numbers should be much higher, while another executive feels relieved to see that the numbers aren't as dismal as they could have been given the state of the economy. He feels relieved. The situation here is the presentation of the financial report, but two different stories have been created.

And here's one more example. Three coworkers who are having lunch together are discussing their boss's most recent financial decision. One of the coworkers, upon hearing the harsh judgment from the other two, states that they are both being very judgmental. That's the situation. Of the two, the first considers the statement for a moment and responds confidently, "I can see why you might think that, but I don't agree with that assessment." The second, however, has an immediate angry reaction: "How dare you call me judgmental. This is just another example of your own inability to hear criticism." Again, the same situation with two different perceptions, one resulting in agitation. That's because there was clearly something else at play for the second person.

For practice, go ahead and make a list of some of the recent situations that you found agitating and resulted in upsetting you. Be as descriptive as possible, but see if you can stick to just the facts. As you do this exercise, you may notice that you begin to feel some agitation. This might confirm your belief that the situation is the source of your agitation. But as we explained and illustrated through

SITUATIONS THAT TAKE PLACE INSIDE

So far we have described situations as events, or physical experiences, since they are easiest to recognize. But situations can also be mental or emotional experiences. For example, you are on your couch, you close your eyes, and a memory that makes you feel happy pops into your head. That's a situation. Or maybe you're walking down the street and you see a dog that reminds you of your pet from childhood, and you suddenly feel sadness over that loss. That's also a situation: walking along, seeing the dog, and experiencing sadness. Maybe you're just running through the day's plans in your head. That's a situation as well. The thoughts we have about these situations weave the stories we tell ourselves. If we are unaware, we think that our stories *are* the situation; we become confused and cannot approach a situation with the clarity we need to be sure that the most harmonious outcome is achieved.

the examples, this is never the case. However, a situation can *trigger* your agitation (that is, "push your button," or, as we like to call it, your I-spot). So where is your agitation coming from? Where does it originate? We'll need to delve deeper and continue to consider that the thoughts (your stories) and the emotions attached to them are resulting in your agitation. Now that you know this, when you feel yourself becoming agitated, ask yourself, *What is it that's upsetting me? Is it my story about the situation? If so, what is the source of that story? Where is that story coming from?* We'll explore this in the next section, "Listening to Your Stories."

LISTENING TO YOUR STORIES

A story is a factual or fictional narrative that our mind plays as a situation unfolds. Stories are the thoughts that rise to the surface of our minds in reaction to the feelings we have about the things that are happening around us. In earlier examples, we identified various situations to illustrate that it isn't the situation that's responsible for our agitation. Rather, what's happening around us activates something within us, and we, in turn, feel something and begin to label what we're feeling and dramatize what we're experiencing. In all cases, the emotional content attached to the story projects itself onto the situation. Let's take a look at the actual stories that accompanied the situations described earlier and are repeated below for your convenience. Notice how the situations are woven into the stories:

◆ Sixty-year-old George is the president of the board of directors for a tremendously successful business on the stock exchange, who has difficulty setting boundaries with people in his personal life.

George says, "I am such a giving and loving person. When it comes to my personal life, why do people keep taking advantage of me? In my business, I would never have succeeded if I let people take advantage of me."

◆ Thirty-year-old Jason, a student, teacher, and writer, is dating a woman who he loves but who does not love him in return, although she does not want to end the relationship.

Jason says, "Although my girlfriend doesn't think she loves me, I know that I am a special person and I have the capacity to win her over."

◆ Twenty-five-year-old Carolina, an accountant, recently divorced her husband who behaved in a verbally abusive manner throughout much of their marriage.

Carolina says, "We had to get a divorce, but I tried so hard to make my marriage work. I can't do anything right. I should have been able to change the relationship. I should have picked the right person to begin with."

◆ Fifty-year-old Michael, a head research scientist who established and runs a research facility, lost his fourth qualified employee in the same number of years and needs to find a replacement.

Michael says, "Qualified employees keep quitting on me! Our society is going down the tubes. We are not teaching people how to commit! Why do I keep hiring people who will not make a long-term commitment to the project?"

◆ Thirty-eight-year-old Cynthia, a successful entrepreneur, has been divorced twice and wants to get married and have children.

Cynthia says, "Why do I keep falling in love with the wrong guy? Why do they keep turning into such creeps? Where is the guy who is a perfect fit for me?"

◆ Forty-two-year-old Mark is a lieutenant colonel in the U.S. Army whose assignment is to assist families of soldiers killed in action. He is twice divorced and lives part-time with his two daughters.

Mark says, "So many emotions come up on the job, and I don't have anyone in my life that I can talk to about them. I wish I had a partner, someone who loves me, someone who looks after me like I look after others."

◆ Fifty-three-year-old William has high blood pressure for which he must take medication.

William says, "I'm going to be on high blood pressure meds my whole life, so why should I even try to make any changes? It doesn't make sense. I'll keep doing what I've always done and get by."

◆ Fifty-six-year-old Stephanie, a successful bodyworker, has a pile of unopened mail, unpaid bills, and unanswered e-mails to attend to.

Stephanie says, "The bills aren't getting paid, and the paperwork is overwhelming. I can't stand to look at the piles. I just don't know how to do this. I have no idea what it takes to run a business. I feel so overwhelmed by it all."

◆ Forty-year-old Keith, a self-employed executive headhunter, spends hours online surfing the Web and making occasional purchases.

Keith says, "My work is very taxing, and I really have to relax, so I surf the Internet and sometimes I don't have enough time left in the day to get my work done. I guess I'm just a slacker."

◆ Thirty-one-year-old Veronica, a yoga instructor, is at odds with her business partner over how to run the business.

Veronica says, "This relationship is too difficult. We're running a yoga center and my partner is always travelling. She is never here and expects me to do all the work, and then she judges me for not doing it right."

◆ Forty-seven-year-old Bethany, a manager of a health-food store, experiences discomfort around the owner of the store, who the employees agree behaves aggressively.

Bethany says, "If I stay out of sight when my boss is around, I won't have to deal with him."

All of the above stories contain subjective information that arises from the clients' *feelings* about the various situations. Because we explained exactly what each client's situation is, you can probably easily separate the situation from the client's story about the event. Jason thinks his girlfriend will fall in love with him if he is romantic enough. This story is a prediction, not a fact. The fact is that he is in a relationship with someone who doesn't love him. Ending it frightens him, and so he clings to his story. (The emotional content of Jason's story, as you probably guessed, is loneliness.) Now, consider Stephanie's story: "I have *no idea* how to run a business . . ." Well, it's highly likely that she does have at least some inkling of how to run a business considering she has one. She is obviously exaggerating and being self-critical. Again, this is not a fact. In Carolina's story, she is blaming her failed marriage on her inability to do things right, which is another exaggeration. When they really looked at the stories they were telling themselves, each of these clients was able to see how their stories were out of balance, rigid, and self-limiting.

Let's consider again the three women on the checkout line mentioned earlier. The first woman had to get home to meet the school bus. She was running out of time, so she left the line and headed home. She was disappointed that she was unable to purchase the groceries, but it passed quickly and she didn't give it much thought thereafter. Her story was, "I need to get home," which was straightforward and based on fact. The second woman was irritated and distracted herself from that irritation first by recalling an upsetting event that occurred that day and then by eating a candy bar and reading a gossip magazine. Her story was, "I was annoyed, but now I'm fine." This story was just a cover up for her uncomfortable feelings. The third woman berated the cashier upon her return and told the cashier that she had a lot of nerve to keep the women waiting. She was hot and her heart was pounding. "I have more important things to do than stand around in line waiting for a stupid cashier," was her story.

So what's the point? The first woman noticed the situation exactly for what it was and recognized that it did not coincide with her goals. She experienced disappointment (an emotion) and then let it go. The other two women, however, experienced the situation but created stories about it. The second woman convinced herself she was fine by eating junk food and reading meaningless words, and the third woman created an agitating story in which she blamed the cashier excessively. The key point here is that even though the first woman experienced an unpleasant emotion (disappointment), she demonstrated the most awareness because she responded to the situation by using the facts: she had to meet the school bus and didn't have time to wait for the cashier to come back. The second woman used a story to help herself "feel fine" about the situation, and the third woman used a story that made her self-righteous and increased her agitation. The second woman probably didn't seem any worse for wear, but if she had been totally aware, she would have recognized and acknowledged her irritation, sat with it for a moment, then breathed into it, became curious about it, and allowed it to dissipate on its own. Then she could have moved on to use the time wisely rather than eating and reading to keep herself distracted. In this way, she would have demonstrated more awareness in a fashion similar to the first woman.

We often blame the situation for being the cause of our agitation, and since it is true that there is a direct link between the two, we need a calm and clear mind to be able to delve deeper into the event to notice that we are out of balance. It takes a considerable amount of practice to gain the ability to step back as if jumping up to a higher level so that we are able to "look down at" or observe ourselves with detachment while still in the situation. Until we are able to observe our behavior from a balanced state of awareness,

Our stories may serve to reject or to validate the feelings we have. For example, someone might say, "Oh, she didn't mean to hurt my feelings, I shouldn't feel this way," thereby negating the validity of his or her feelings without really addressing the emotion. Someone else might say, "Her words were harsh; how dare she say those things to me? Doesn't she know she hurt my feelings? Why would she do that? How rude of her!" thereby turning the emotion into anger. Either way, these stories are not allowing the person to simply experience the feeling of being hurt.

we will continue to feel victimized by the many situations in life that don't meet our expectations.

If the third woman, who was agitated and stuck in the thought that it was the cashier's fault, could see herself through the eyes of the people around her, she might actually be surprised by her over-reaction to the situation. If she could be objective enough to notice that her agitation did nothing to resolve or improve the situation, she might be able to take a deep breath and get curious about why she was having such an emotional reaction to this particular situation.

It is important to acknowledge and be completely aware that

there can be a profound distortion and difference between our story and the actual situation. Here's a good example: You walk into a room. You have no idea what was going on in the room before you got there. You look around at the people and they are all frowning. You immediately begin making up a story: *I shouldn't have come in. They don't want me here.* You've interpreted the frowns on their faces to mean that you are unwanted, but their frowns might have absolutely nothing to do with you.

This is a simplified way of looking at the many different situations that occur in life and how we distort their meaning. Making up a story reduces your awareness and creates imbalance. It causes tension, tightness, and rigidity; in other words, it reduces your flexibility. It closes the door on all of the other possibilities available to you in any situation.

THE TYPES OF THOUGHTS THAT MAKE UP STORIES

When you begin telling yourself a story about a situation, you want to get curious about what type or types of thoughts are making up your stories. In order to do this, it's important to understand that stories are actually made up of a string of thoughts. A thought typi-cally only lasts a few seconds; however, the space between thoughts for most people is so small that the thoughts appear to be an unend-ing stream. Therefore, a story is actually a long series of individual thoughts packed closely together. Every single thought (and its cor-responding emotion) that passes across the screen of your mind can be placed into one of five categories: accurate, inaccurate, memory, fantasy, and blank (without content). Let's take a closer look at each of these categories.

When we experience an event, our mind immediately produces a corresponding thought. That's its job. For example, when I see Radha walking with packages in her hand, my mind immediately thinks that she would appreciate a helping hand. If the thought or story is accu-rate, then she replies in the affirmative.

An *accurate thought* is one without any distortion. It reaches the appropriate conclusion regarding the event that just occurred either in our inner world (such as recognizing when we feel a specific emo-tion or remembering that we have an appointment) or in the outer world (recognizing a friend solely by the sound of her voice). Observ-ing events as they are *without distortion* falls into the category of accu-rate perception. You look at a palm tree that is planted in your front yard and your story is in harmony with the event: *that is a palm tree.* Whenever our story or thought is congruous with the situation, it is accurate.

The second type of thought is an *inaccurate thought*. These thoughts cause problems in a person's life. We make inaccurate conclusions, due to either misinformation or a false impression. For example, my client William told me how he made a fool out of himself when he yelled at an employee for talking on his cell phone during company time. When William saw the person on the phone, his mind made the inaccurate conclusion that the employee was cheating his company by making a personal call. If William had taken the time to ask, he would have been told that William's partner had already given the employee permission to call his wife to find out how his daughter was doing after a minor outpatient operation.

When we perceive an event incorrectly, when it does not represent the facts of the situation, it is called an inaccurate story. Therefore, William's conclusion about the situation (the employee was taking an unscheduled break) was partially true, but it lead him to create an inaccurate story because he did not have all the information. No one can ever have *all* the information regarding *any* situation. For this reason, many people make inaccurate decisions based on accurate, but incomplete, stories. (Accurate and inaccurate stories are one of the reasons we have lawyers and judges in our society.)

The third type of thought is *fantasy* or a series of thoughts that are created by our imagination. Let's say that William begins to create a

story in his mind that the employee is plotting with a friend on the phone to steal items in his warehouse. While his employee is merely concerned about the welfare of his child, William is imagining that a criminal act is being planned.

Imagination has the ability to create something in our mind that does not match reality. Fantasy is the source of creativity. It is the stuff of fairy tales, fiction novels, and all of the original ideas that give birth to new inventions. However, if we are not aware that we are fantasizing, it can most certainly wreak havoc on the stories we create in our mind.

Our ability to create fantasy stories or use our imagination is always determined, and ultimately limited, by the contents of our mind. In William's hypothetical case, the fact that he thought his employee was stealing wasn't based on any evidence; it was nothing more than a figment of his imagination. Therefore, his inability to trust his employee stemmed from his issue (more about this in Chapter 3) and manifested itself in the form of a fantasy: *my employee is planning to steal from me,* even though, to William's knowledge, that had never happened.

Making our decisions based on fantasy can lead us into disastrous consequences in both our personal and professional lives, but nonetheless, it is a common tactic used to avoid situations that involve unpleasant or conflicting emotions. For example, how often do we fantasize about the future rather than deal with a challenging situation in the present? Similarly, many people stay in a situation based on past experiences rather than allow relationships and situations to evolve naturally over the course of time. This brings us to the next type of thought: memory.

Memory is recalling a previous situation or story with its accompanying emotion and either matching it or projecting it onto the present moment. The positive part of memory is that we do not have to spend the same amount of time to relearn a lesson, remember someone's name, or recall a skill like how to drive a car. Imagine how little we would get accomplished every day if we had to repeat the process of learning where to insert the key, how to start the car, and so on. Our world would be chaotic and possibly come to a standstill. But because we have memory—the ability to hold a fact, event, or specific skill-set in the storage area of our mind—we can access an entire library of information in a second. It is thanks to our memory that we are able to function in the world. Think for a moment about senior citizens whose short-term memory becomes severely impaired; they are unable to continue to lead productive, independent lives. Regardless of age or circumstance, a person who does not have a properly functioning memory is condemned to a life of complete dependence upon others.

Now that we understand the importance of memory, we should also consider what happens when we remember something that isn't true. The downside of memory is that if we relive an event enough times in our mind, we soon believe it to be fact. Repeating a thought such as *I am such an idiot!* deepens it in the memory banks in our subconscious mind. Maybe someone said this to us in anger when we were children, yet after years of repeating it, it can become embedded in our operating system. It doesn't matter if it's true or not; we experience it many times during the day as a memory and believe that it is a truth. When Mark's child forgets to make her bed in the morning, he becomes frustrated because it means he has to do it himself. This triggers an old childhood memory about how no one was there for him, and as a result he becomes angry with his daughter and tells her she is lazy. Rather than responding to the situation in an appropriate manner (having a loving conversation with his daughter about responsibility and the importance of making her bed), he reacts to the memory of how he had to do everything for himself as a child. If this unconscious behavior continues, it may ultimately result in his daughter not wanting to spend time with him, and this becomes a self-fulfilling prophecy for Mark.

> Memory serves as a means of retaining important information that is still somehow relevant to our life. We recall memories because our mind has deemed them pertinent to our present circumstances.

Another important thing to note is that memories often distort what actually happened, and in some cases, the events recalled may not have even happened at all. For example, Radha and I have entirely different recollections of the day we met. Nearly forty years have passed since then, and at this point it is obviously impossible to determine whose memory is accurate. We joke about it often: after many years of marriage, we are still amazed at how many things we believe are true may not have happened as we recall.

Memory-based stories are helpful if they further our ability to navigate our life successfully. But just because we remember something, there is no guarantee that it is the complete truth. For each memory we hold in our mind, there is a corresponding emotional experience. Since every memory is attached to an emotional response or reaction, it is easy to conclude that if you are uncomfortable with the emotion, you will have a negative reaction to any situation that reminds you of that past event and emotion.

Using memory to your advantage requires a high level of awareness because one must discern whether a particular memory connects us more closely to the situation at hand (such as remembering a friend's face) or pushes us further away (holding a grudge against someone for something that happened in the past). Living in the past limits our ability to grow, learn, and explore life fully. If Mark does not recognize the distortion of his memory every time he is upset with his daughter's performance, an unseen ghost from the past will finally push his child away.

The fifth category or type of thought is a "no-story," a *blank thought,* a thought that grabs our attention but has no content; it is completely empty. This is a rather strange type of thought. Why would we even have unproductive, blank, empty thoughts? Maybe it's the universe's way of providing us with a moment of rest. Whatever the reason, virtually everyone can remember a moment when they were just staring out into space without a specific idea in their head. For example, I remember back in first grade how I would use every opportunity to get up out of my wooden desk to sharpen my pencil (it was the only way I could stretch my legs). While sharpening what might have been my tenth pencil, I just stared out the window without a thought in my mind—"spacing out" as my teacher called it when she sent me to the principal's office on more than one occasion. This is an example of the blank thought. It is a wave of nothingness, yet we are aware that it isn't sleep, and when someone asks, "What are you thinking?" the honest answer is *I was not thinking of anything.* Women are notorious for asking this question, and men are notorious for answering with this response. It's good for both sexes to know that it's actually possible to be thinking of nothing.

The activity of the mind (or thought), which is devoid of meaning and content, is very similar to, but not the same as, sleep. Unlike the thoughts that have content—such as a childhood memory, a fantasy about having a successful career or relationship, or even an accurate or inaccurate thought whose content includes an analysis of a current situation—the wave of nothing is much different.

When we think *about* something, there is a change that takes place in our mind. In other words, we react or respond. And at the completion of that thought, we are different than we were before we had the thought. An example of this is if you are reading a sentence in a book that results in the creation of an insightful idea. You are changed by that thought. There is continuity between the information you just read and the moments that follow. Not so with this fifth type of thought. No change takes place; you are the same person after this *thought of nothing* that you were before it occurred.

> A story must include at least one of the five types of thoughts, but it could quite easily include several of them—and perhaps even all five!

I was told that my teacher asked me why I was sharpening so many pencils. The story goes that I wore a dazed expression and had no satisfying answer. The thought of nothing was happening as I was grinding the pencil down to its eraser, yet I had no awareness of performing the deed. You can think of this thought as the mind *drifting* away with no one there to pay attention to the direction it is taking. A drifting mind can occur at anytime, without warning and without cognition. Have you ever arrived at your destination and realized you have no memory of having gotten off the bus or parking the car? It was comforting for me to learn from my study of meditation and Eastern philosophy that these types of thoughts are part of a much larger understanding of how the mind works. (For more on this, consider reading *Raja Yoga* listed in the Suggested Reading section on page 191.)

Now that you are aware that your thoughts can be categorized into types of thoughts—and therefore stories with varying degrees of accuracy, inaccuracy, fantasy, memory-based thoughts, and blank thoughts—you are in a better position to be curious about the thoughts that you use to create the stories about various situations.

HOW INFLEXIBILITY IMPACTS YOUR STORIES

As described in Chapter 1, flexibility is one of the three skills you need to successfully navigate the experiences in your life. Keep this in mind when examining your stories. Take a really close look at them to see if they are so deeply ingrained in your mind that you cannot waver from them. For example, if you're pushing, judging, or trying to make a situation be exactly the way you want it to be, you are stuck in an inflexible stance. We've all been in a situation where we are having a discussion that suddenly verges on an argument. We have our position, and we're going to stay in that position because we want the other person to "get it." We're stuck in that. We don't want to move. We want the other person to understand where we are coming from; we want to convince them that we are right. In a case like this, we are projecting onto the situation what we want it to be. We are

rigid in our position. In fact, we might "snap." This is not the outcome we want. We do not want to blow up at the other person simply because they don't think like we do.

For example, when Veronica learned she was reacting to her business partner rather than responding with awareness, and that her reaction prevented her from even understanding her partner's position,

she started to really pay attention to what she was experiencing physically, mentally, and emotionally. Physically, she noticed the rigidity in
her body—the tightness in her chest and jaw, the shallow breathing,
the feeling of wanting to cry, and shaking in
her solar plexus. With practice, she learned
to pause, take deep breaths, and relax her
shoulders and jaw before responding to
her partner. She learned to recognize that
she had an inflexible story screaming inside
her mind: her partner was not listening to
her or hearing her point of view. To correct

> *Taking an inflexible
> stance during a
> contrary conversation
> often leads to tension
> in some part of your
> physical body.*

this, she made a decision to focus on what her partner was saying.
This shift from self-absorbed reaction to making herself available gave
her a much-needed change in her pattern of thinking, which allowed
her to understand (although she did not agree with) her partner's
perspective.

If we're not aware that we're being rigid, we're going to push away
information that might be important for our growth. So, once again,
awareness is essential. Really pay attention to your flexibility or lack of
flexibility in your positions on various issues. For example, our client
Irving felt pressured by his mother-in-law's insistence that he, his wife,
and his kids attend Shabbat dinner at her home every Friday night.
Irving's story was that it was no fun, he didn't get anything out of it,
and that his mother-in-law was controlling him and judging him. He
rigidly refused to even consider that it could be a nice way to spend
time with his family. His thinking regarding this situation was so
inflexible that as Shabbat approached each Friday, he would tense up
and clench his jaw, which would then manifest as a tension headache.
Then he'd spend the entire evening uncomfortable and upset. When
the connection between his rigid thinking and his headache was
pointed out to him, he eventually learned to relax enough to consider
his mother-in-law's request from a new, more flexible perspective. He
attended some of the Friday night dinners, but others he did not.

As illustrated by Irving's and Veronica's examples, if you're inflexible in your belief systems, you will also find some inflexibility—some rigidity—in your body. Your brain is sending and receiving signals all the time; it transforms your inflexible thought patterns and transmits them throughout your body. If you are mentally rigid, the power of that rigidity will eventually manifest in your body. This is the mind-body connection in action. The remarkable thing with the mind-body connection is that a rigid thought has a specific resonance that will affect corresponding areas of the body. Your body has to compensate for these inflexible thoughts, so the next thing you know, you have a stiff back or stiff shoulders, or the muscles in the back of your legs are shortening and tightening. Of course, how and what you think isn't the only cause of rigidity or inflexibility in the body. Other situations and circumstances also come into play. However, if you show inflexibility in how you handle your interactions with others and within yourself, it is going to show up in your body. If you doubt this, pay

A WAY TO STAY FLEXIBLE

A helpful strategy for staying flexible is to practice taking in *all incoming information* as possibly accurate before making a judgment that is not true. This is more difficult than it sounds because many of us have become so accustomed to believing our thoughts about how the world around us operates. Whenever we come into contact with information that seems to contradict our worldview, we instantly snap to the judgment: *This isn't true.* Similarly, when we encounter an idea or situation that confirms our preexisting notions, a different judgment (but just as quick) happens: *Yes, this is true.* But if we can learn to pause before making these judgments and just sit with new information before arriving at a conclusion, we will often be surprised by how our environment is giving us important feedback about how to respond to the situation.

closer attention next time you are so set in your position on something that you begin to tense up.

The key to staying flexible in relationships is being able to take in information—whether verbal, nonverbal, emotional, or mental—without immediately judging it or reacting to it. Too often we jump to conclusions because we have a preconceived notion about what the person is communicating. This also falls under the category of inflex-ibility. For example, if we're concerned about having enough money, negotiating a raise from our employer might be difficult because every bit of feedback has to be filtered through the idea *I don't have enough money*. This atti-tude can cause us to miss out on important information because we're always on the defensive around our boss. Our reaction is inflexible, rigid, and fixed. Similarly, in a romantic relationship, feelings of poor self-esteem might cause us to seek affirmation from our partner. Rather than sharing honestly with our mate, we may act in ways that we *think* will elicit his or her approval and/or affection. If an inflexible person doesn't get the desired response, then he or she will take it as a judgment about his or her failure in the relationship.

> *Every situation and story has emotional content connected to it, even if you are not aware of it.*

In both cases, a lack of flexibility can cause tremendous difficulty because it forces us to filter or reject all the feedback we get from oth-ers. When this feedback matches our expectations, we feel good; when it doesn't, we become defensive and reactive. These filters are nothing more than stories, so the essential step to maintaining a flex-ible relationship is to respond to the situation rather than reacting to the filter/story. An interesting side note on flexibility is how we some-times view long-term relationships as stagnant things that will always remain the same. We need to be flexible enough in our perception of relationships to allow the natural changes that occur between people, especially in long-term relationships such as those between parent and child, childhood friends, or husband and wife.

Stephanie's Experience

AN INFLEXIBLE STANCE

 Stephanie is an excellent bodyworker who receives much praise from her clients. Overall she is pleased with that aspect of her business. However, when it comes to handling the financial side of running her own business, she becomes stubborn and rigid. She has told herself the same story—*I am terrible with money*—so often that her finances have taken on an ugly life of their own.

When she arrives at home and sees the piles of unopened mail or thinks about the bills that must be processed, she tenses up. For a moment she considers dealing with the piles, but then tells herself, "I'm not going to make any headway, so why bother?" This doesn't make her feel any better, and so she begins berating herself for being so "bad" at managing money, and she tenses up even more.

To drown out her unforgiving inner critic, she fills a bowl with her favorite comfort food and takes a familiar place on the sofa and turns on the TV. Thus, she continues a ritual of distraction in an attempt to zone out and avoid her uncomfortable feelings. In this state, Stephanie is so rigid that she cannot even see her own successes.

As part of her work, Stephanie was asked to practice her fifteen-minute personal program that included the Waterfall Flexibility Exercise (see page 58) each evening upon returning from work. Not surprisingly, after engaging in her program, she eased up on her harsh opinion of her abilities to handle her finances and felt less of a need to distract herself. She agreed to spend a few minutes each night sorting mail and taking care of her financial obligations before focusing on a healthy choice for dinner and an evening activity.

❧ The Waterfall Flexibility Exercise ❧

Do not practice this exercise if you have high blood pressure, glaucoma, or herniated discs.

Your body is an important feedback mechanism that needs to be tuned up regularly. Since we have been stressing the importance of flexibility in this chapter, this exercise is designed to increase your flexibility on the physical level, which in turn will increase your flexibility on the mental level. Throughout this and similar exercises, try to identify any muscles that feel tight, bring your awareness there, and consciously begin to soften and relax those muscles. (This is also applicable to your mind. If you put your awareness there, you can soften and relax any rigid, inflexible beliefs.)

Whenever you're getting uptight, a part of your body is going to tighten. That's how it works. The brain receives a message, amplifies it, and sends it to specific cells that resonate in harmony with that particular thought even though it may create disharmony in the body. Over a period of time, this is going to tighten muscles in your body. For instance, if you hold tension in your abdominal muscles, your digestive system can be affected. If you continually clench your jaw, it may result in headaches. The brain's communication system can be positively affected when you learn how to engage awareness for your physical, mental, and emotional well-being. When you learn how to disrupt negative communication to the brain, the positive effects will be felt in your body. Practicing this exercise will get things moving again.

Stand on the floor with your feet parallel and breathe in deeply. Experience your spine lengthening upward as you inhale, becoming aware of the space between your vertebrae. Then, exhale slowly through the nose, doubling the exhalation, and notice that your spine begins to compress. On each inhalation, you get taller, and on each exhalation you get shorter. Depending on how flexible you are, if you are forty-five years of age or older, you can actually increase/decrease your height by an inch or an inch and a half!

Now bring your hands up overhead. Stretch your arms up toward the ceiling, keeping your feet flat on the floor. Create as much space between your feet and your fingertips as you can. As you inhale, stretch your arms upward. Take several deep breaths. Now stretch a little higher with your right arm, leaning a bit to the right. As you do, lift your left heel—not your left foot. So, right arm up, left heel up. Now switch to the other side and stretch a little higher with your left arm, leaning a bit to the left. As you do, lift up your right heel—not your right foot. So, left arm up, right heel up. This causes a diagonal stretch throughout your body. When you are feeling tired, this is an excellent exercise to do instead of turning to sugar or coffee for a quick pick-me-up. Practice this technique often.

Now, with both feet flat on the floor, stretch both arms equally, then let your arms crash down to the side of your body. Slightly bend your legs at the knees, drop your head down, relax your arms, and begin to roll down very slowly— head, neck, shoulders, and back rolling down toward the floor, vertebra by vertebra. If you experience any pain in your back as you're bending down, either bend your knees more, stop the exercise completely, or hold on to your thighs, and then let your arms hang limply. If your back is flexible, lock your knees and hang. You're just limply hanging. Take several deep, slow breaths. Think about where your muscles are tight. Where are you inflexible? (Don't compare your flexibility to others. You are simply trying to improve your own flexibility; you are not competing with anyone.)

Your head is below your heart, you're getting fresh blood to your brain, and the muscles that support your spine, hips, and legs are being stretched. You can hold this position for up to five minutes. When you're ready to stand upright again, unlock your knees and very slowly begin to roll up, vertebra by vertebra, tucking your pelvis under and keeping your head down until the last moment. (If your back feels strained, bend your knees more and hold on to your thighs as you roll up.) Put your shoulders back and your head up, and you're done. There is no limit to how often you repeat this exercise.

❧ *Experience for the Road* ❦

Spend some time in a public place, such as a park or a mall, where you know you'll see a lot of people. Find a comfortable spot and watch the situations around you as they unfold. What are you observing? Come up with stories for each of the situations. For example, if you are in the mall, make up a story about a shopper, such as, *That woman is shopping for a gift for her boyfriend.* It doesn't matter if it's true. Just have fun with it. Let your mind play with this and have fun with this experience. Simply be aware that you are creating a story around an event: a woman is shopping. If you are at the park and you see a man on his cell phone, make up a story, such as, *That man is on the phone with his son and is upset because his son didn't do his homework quickly enough and can't make it to the park.* It doesn't have to make sense. Just get used to the fact that situations always spawn stories. When you've spent some time doing this, take this experience to another level by looking at what types of stories you develop. You might very well notice that there's a pattern to your stories, which will provide further insight into how you operate.

Part 2 of this Experience for the Road activity takes a bit more sensitivity and awareness. Begin exactly as you did in the first exercise. Observe a situation, allowing your mind the freedom to make up a story. Now, notice if there are any physical sensations (feelings in your body) and emotions connected to this event. There may not be. However, since most situations set off a barrage of thoughts, and thoughts create emotional reactions or responses, this is a perfect exercise to practice noticing your emotional states of consciousness. You can ask yourself questions like, *Is there an emotion attached to this story? Does my story about the situation include any basic emotions, such as anger, sadness, or joy? Are my stories negative or positive? Do they place one person in the victim role?* Just be aware, without any sense that there is a right or wrong story or observation. Even if you do not have an answer, simply asking yourself these questions prepares you to be more aware the next time you get agitated and have a reaction to a particular situation. You are practicing being more aware of the emotional content of your stories.

There's one more thing to note about this activity: if you feel a strong emotion, be sure to take note of the specifics in the story you created. There may be significance to why you reacted the way you did. For example, if you see two people arguing, it could bring up a strong emotion. Notice it and pay attention to the physical location of the emotion. This will come in handy later on in the program. In the process of having fun with this exercise, you are developing the ability to "jump out of the system." This means you'll be able to step back with more awareness and notice your own stories. Whether they are accurate or inaccurate is not important right now. What's more important is that you know that the mind is a storyteller and that you are not the mind or its stories.

As with everything else on this journey, separating the story from the situation begins with becoming more aware of what's going on inside of us as well as outside of us. The situations that occur in life are what life is all about. Things happen, we have emotional responses, and we experience the ups and downs of life. This is wonderful. What's also wonderful is that as human beings we are self-reflective. We can actually step back and analyze, "Oh, look at that. I'm getting upset/agitated. Isn't that interesting?" A simple comment, one that had absolutely no malicious intent, can stir up things inside us, things that are so uncomfortable that we feel we must push them away or cover them up with all sorts of stories. There's something deeper at work here. There are buttons being pushed that operate on such a deep level that we often don't know what's just hit us. In cases like this, we need to consider the subconscious mechanisms at work in our reactions; in other words, we need to discover our hidden issues, the subject of Chapter 3.

The Hidden Factor
Revealing the Issue

Self-esteem is more than merely feeling positive about yourself. In order to truly love yourself and be content with your life, you must identify the barriers holding you back. Each of us carries self-limiting beliefs that prevent us from navigating life successfully.

—GARY AND RADHA BELLO

Having separated the story from the situation, we are now ready to make a giant leap forward. We are going to look at the emotions beneath our stories. An emotion is the experiencing of life. We are empathetic beings, and we're designed to feel. Many of the emotions we experience are connected to specific thoughts. All of our stories carry with them emotional reactions or responses. If you're in complete harmony with your experience, you will have an emotional *response* to the situation, and whatever that response is, it will be perfect, whether that response is anger to an injustice or joy over something wonderful. You will respond appropriately.

However, if you are in *reaction*, the past has been activated and you are literally re-acting what happened previously. If the thinking mode is on, you are one step removed from experiencing the situation directly because you are experiencing it through the filter of memory, and that emotional experience will be corrupted in some way. You will be unable to deal with that new situation without preconceived notions that distort your perspective. In our practice, we are working toward being able to *respond* to situations without the interference of our limiting filters.

In this chapter, we're going to examine what it is that explodes inside of our mind that prevents us from being completely present to every situation in our life. First, let's take another quick look at the difference between an emotional response and an emotional reaction. Allow me to share a personal story with you to illustrate this: My mother died two years ago, and my father asked me to give the eulogy for my mom at the crematorium. I felt sad—a deep, profound sadness—but not agitated. My aunt, on the other hand, was totally distraught and kept crying out, "What am I going to do? How am I going to go on?" The difference between my response to my mother's death and my aunt's reaction to my mother's death is that one of us was coming from an imbalanced place. My concern was for myself, yes, but also for my father, my sisters, and most of all for my mother, whom I had been there for as she passed. My sadness was deep, but I was able to maintain concern for others and was able to respond as needed. My aunt, meanwhile, was mostly concerned with her loss and how she would get by without my mother. So, in a nutshell, the difference between imbalanced and balanced emotional responses is the difference between self-absorption and selflessness.

What is it that colors our stories about the events that take place around us? In Chapter 1, we used the metaphor of a virus in our operating system, the virus that becomes activated when certain buttons are pushed. These viruses prevent us from navigating life successfully because they interfere with our perception of situations. They cloud our judgment. When the virus is active, we are in "issue activation."

We all have some version of this malware, and if we are aware enough and brave enough to admit it, then we are in a position to deactivate it with the right intentions. The only variable here is how often we operate with the virus running rampant in our system. Some people are running with the virus active all the time. They are always in issue-activated mode. For example, William has a successful business, but the recent economic downturn was the catalyst that activated his trouble with trust, and now he walks around suspicious of his employees and reacts to things they say and do through an erroneous filter of suspicion. Yet, on the other hand, as a businessman he has to be aware of the possibility that people could steal from him. Because the virus is active, he may even behave this way with his family, friends, and acquaintances. He can't see the situation clearly anymore because he is operating through a clouded perception.

Sadly, there are many people in life who are in this reactive mode all the time. Operating from this issue-activated place requires a tremendous amount of physical and mental energy to keep it from interfering with normal daily activities, and in this way it causes imbalances in other areas of one's life, inviting *dis-ease*. Other people operate from this issue-activated

Is•sue (noun)
1. *subject of concern*
2. *main subject*
3. *problem or difficulty*
4. *source of flow*
5. *discharge from wound*
6. *self-limiting belief*

place less frequently or in varying degrees. William's partner, for example, may also have trust issues, but it's only a certain type of event that arouses his feelings of mistrust. In some cases, he is able to *respond* as called for by a situation and in other cases he may *react* to some perceived wrongdoing.

So, what exactly are these viruses? They are the *erroneous core beliefs,* the issues that reside just below the surface of our conscious mind, in what is called the subconscious. We've listed them on the next page so that you can familiarize yourself with them. At first, you might be surprised that there are only a handful of them, but when you examine them closely, you'll recognize their universality. And with some serious, honest, and heartfelt self-reflection, you will discover that you do relate to one or more of them on a very visceral level.

Don't try to convince yourself that you *shouldn't* feel these things by telling yourself more stories. These aren't logical beliefs, so don't try to intellectualize them. That's why we call them viruses.

- ◆ I am not safe.
- ◆ I am alone.
- ◆ I am not good enough.
- ◆ I am unfulfilled.

- ◆ I am not heard.
- ◆ I am unable to trust.
- ◆ I am unacceptable.
- ◆ I don't have enough time.

WHAT EMOTIONS CAUSE YOU DISCOMFORT?

To get to the heart of our agitation and deactivate that virus in our operating system, we need to begin to develop the necessary software by increasing our awareness of our emotions, especially by identifying the emotions that make us the most uncomfortable. You know, the ones that kind of shake you when you experience them, the ones that you *feel* in your body. Maybe for you it's sadness, disappointment, or discouragement; maybe there's shame, anger, or frustration. Whatever the case may be, really think about it and ask yourself, *What emotions make me feel uncomfortable?* (If you have trouble identifying emotions in the first place, go back to the inset on page 14, and try to recall instances where you felt those feelings.) Once you've identified the emotions you feel uncomfortable experiencing, you will be tuned in to essential information. Your discomfort is an important clue for eventually removing the doubt and cloudiness that come from whatever it is that causes that uncomfortable reaction within you.

In the course of a typical day, we experience a myriad of emotional reactions and responses to situations. In fact, emotions make up the majority of our life. Every step we take and every experience in our life invites us to feel, to experience the moment fully, to be forced into a physical sensation that moves us to notice the emotion. However, if we are unable to have a comfortable, balanced response to a particular emotion—due either to improper exposure or practice—we suffer the consequences. If we are not comfortable with an emotion, we are compelled to avoid it at all costs, which limits our availability to experiences that include these emotions, though this oftentimes happens subconsciously. However, if we have enough awareness, we are able to notice the emotions that we are most uncomfortable experiencing, and once we are aware of them, we can shine a light on the strategies we've developed to avoid them.

For example, if a person is uncomfortable with embarrassment, he will avoid situations in which he might feel exposed, such as a public speaking opportunity. If someone is uncomfortable with anger, she might avoid engaging in a debate over something she feels passionately about. If a person is uncomfortable with feelings of confrontation, he might let someone take advantage of him. Remember Jason? In his case, his discomfort concerned the feeling of loneliness. He avoided this feeling by composing love poems where he romanticized the feelings, making them more palatable. Once he realized that he was shying away from loneliness and saw that the poetry was distracting him from it, he was able to face the loneliness he was feeling and simply experience it.

It takes a concentrated effort to recognize that we are running away and/or distracting ourselves from an emotion, but the benefit of doing this is to become more emotionally available to new opportunities and experiences. It's worth the effort.

There are variations of the erroneous core beliefs and multiple combinations. Though not everyone will readily admit it to others or to themselves, we all have some level of insecurity. If you don't relate to one or more of the statements on page 66, try these on for size:

Variations of Erroneous Core Beliefs

There's no one here for me.

I have to do it myself.

No one's listening to me.

Nobody pays attention to me.

It's not safe.

I am a terrible person.

I feel empty.

People can't be trusted.

There's not enough time.

I suck.

I am awful.

I can't speak up.

I screw up everything.

I'll never find anyone.

I am unlovable.

I always wait till the last minute.

I can't do anything right.

The world is a scary place.

People are mean.

No one understands me.

There's something missing from my life.

Nothing good ever happens to me.

Nobody loves me.

Everything goes wrong.

It's a cruel world.

I missed my calling.

I always feel rushed.

I am going to explode.

I am afraid.

I am uncertain.

I am vulnerable.

I am helpless.

I am not valuable.

I am unable to fix it.

I am no good.

I can't make it work.

I am unsuccessful.

I am inferior.

I am worthless.

I am invisible.

I am insignificant.

I am plain and dull.

I am not special.

I don't matter.

I am unworthy.

I am not interesting.

I don't know.

I am always wrong.

I can't understand.

I am never understood.

I am in the wrong place.

I am a mistake.

I don't belong.

I am unwanted.

I am unwelcome.

I don't fit in anywhere.

I don't exist.

I am nothing.

I am unimportant.

I should not be here.

I am a nobody.

I am left out.

I am unsuitable.

I am uninteresting.

I don't matter to anyone.

It's my fault.

I did something wrong.

I am bad.

I am not whole.

I am imperfect.

I am unattractive.

I am disgusting.

I am flawed.

I am stupid.

I am awkward.

I am slow.

I am ugly.

I am fat.

I am useless.

I am missing something.

I am out of control.

I can't make myself clear.

I am mistaken.

I am unbalanced.

I will fail.

I am a failure.

I don't deserve to be loved.

I don't deserve to be cared for.

I don't deserve anything.

Nothing I do is enough.

There's something wrong
  with me.

I can't do it.

I won't do it.

I am a victim.

I am weak.

I am powerless.

I am ineffective.

I don't have any choice.

I am unworthy of love.

I am a loser.

I am inadequate.

I can't say "no."

In order to truly love ourselves and to navigate life through the experience of enlightening moments, we must be willing to identify the obstacles that get in the way and keep us rooted in patterns that do not serve us.

Let's take a look at the clients we discussed earlier through the presentation of their situations and their accompanying stories. You have probably figured out by now that each of their stories had an issue activation associated with it. Most of the time, these people function quite well in the world. Now, let's take a look at each of these client's erroneous core beliefs, which they discovered through self-reflection and the methods in this program. Remember, none of the erroneous core beliefs are based on reality, but rather on faulty programming. Also keep in mind that different people will often have different reactions even if they share the same issue. It's also important to note that most people have a combination of erroneous core beliefs that can become activated singularly or in different combinations according to the situation. Let's take a look at some specific examples. The situations and stories have been repeated here for your convenience.

George

◆ Sixty-year-old George is the president of the board of directors for a tremendously successful business on the stock exchange, who has difficulty setting boundaries with people in his personal life.

George says, "I am such a giving and loving person. When it comes to my personal life, why do people keep taking advantage of me? In my business, I would never have succeeded if I let people take advantage of me."

George's issue is *I am alone.* When activated, this issue prevents him from setting boundaries in his personal life and being truthful about his needs. He has developed a supersensitivity for knowing what people need and goes out of his way to provide it for them. *There's no one here for me* is a common theme among people with the issue *I am alone*. Oftentimes, these people are not tuned in to their own needs, but are extremely sensitive to the needs of others. You'll find a great number of people with this issue in the helping professions, but that's certainly not a prerequisite for having this issue.

Jason

◆ Thirty-year-old Jason, a student, teacher, and writer, is dating a woman who he loves but who does not love him in return, although she does not want to end the relationship.

Jason says, "Although my girlfriend doesn't think she loves me, I know that I am a special person and I have the capacity to win her over."

For Jason, *I am alone* causes him to try to change, transform, or manipulate a situation in an effort to attract others to be there for him, as he does by romanticizing his relationship with his girlfriend. We've all heard the saying "People who need people are the luckiest people in the world," and that's a romantic way to look at it. Someone with the issue *I am alone* will often go to great lengths to keep people close by and may alienate people with their neediness.

Carolina

◆ Twenty-five-year-old Carolina, an accountant, recently divorced her husband who behaved in a verbally abusive manner throughout much of their marriage.

Carolina says, "We had to get a divorce, but I tried so hard to make my marriage work. I can't do anything right. I should have been able to change the relationship. I should have picked the right person to begin with."

Carolina's issue is *I am not good enough*. This causes her to frame her divorce as a personal failure because she feels flawed and blames herself for her inadequacies as a wife. People who feel they are lacking something are often very hard on themselves even when they've done everything "right." They have difficulty accepting a job well done and will search out a flaw to confirm their erroneous belief about themselves.

Michael

♦ Fifty-year-old Michael, a head research scientist who established and runs a research facility, lost his fourth qualified employee in the same number of years and needs to find a replacement.

Michael says, "Qualified employees keep quitting on me! Our society is going down the tubes. We are not teaching people how to commit! Why do I keep hiring people who will not make a long-term commitment to the project?"

Michael's issue is *I can't trust anyone*. This causes him to treat people with a high degree of suspicion, and in his particular case, he confronts them, making them feel uncomfortable under his unwarranted scrutiny. Michael's attitude that it's "my way or the highway" blocked the creative expression of the research scientists he employed. That's why they kept quitting. People with the issue *I can't trust anyone* are often on high alert. They have difficulty letting people in, and if they do end up letting someone in and getting hurt, it is proof to them that *no one* can be trusted. When this issue is activated, the person will usually be confrontational and controlling as a way to distract themselves from feeling.

Cynthia

♦ Thirty-eight-year-old Cynthia, a successful entrepreneur, has been divorced twice and wants to get married and have children.

Cynthia says, "Why do I keep falling in love with the wrong guy?

Why do they keep turning into such creeps? Where is the guy who is a perfect fit for me?"

Cynthia's issues are *I am not good enough* and *there's not enough time.* This causes her to seek validation from men and jump into relationships too quickly. If she finds a man to love her and marry her, she believes this will prove her worth. First, though, a potential mate must pass her scrutiny. However, if he is interested in *her,* he will have to prove to her that he is perfect.

Seeking validation from others to quell the issue of *I'm not good enough* is a common thread for a lot of people. This is especially true in our society where people tie their self-worth to their accomplishments. This type of self-worth is fleeting, however, since people with this issue are always striving to accomplish something even greater. *It's never enough!* In Cynthia's case, *there's not enough time* makes her feel as if she must rush headlong into relationships despite the fact that her other issue may be interfering with her judgment regarding the best course of action. This is not uncommon among people with this issue.

Mark

◆ Forty-two-year-old Mark is a lieutenant colonel in the U.S. Army whose assignment is to assist families of soldiers killed in action. He is twice divorced and lives part-time with his two daughters.

Mark says, "So many emotions come up on the job, and I don't have anyone in my life that I can talk to about it. I wish I had a partner, someone who loves me, someone who looks after me like I look after others."

For Mark, the *I am alone* issue causes him to feel he must do everything himself and no one can do anything as well as he does. Due to these high expectations, he is constantly judging others and becoming upset when they do not do things according to his needs. In relationships with women, this leads to an inability to expose his vulnerabilities, and therefore, he cannot maintain an intimate relationship.

People with this issue who feel they must do everything them-selves often push people away because they don't know how to accept assistance. If they do accept assistance, they often have high expectations of what that assistance should entail because they know exactly how they would handle it. This obviously causes disappoint-ment, because people can rarely live up to other people's expectations of them. This usually causes others to feel as if there is something wrong with them.

William

◆ Fifty-three-year-old William has high blood pressure for which he must take medication.

William says, "I'm going to be on high blood pressure meds my whole life so why should I even try to make any changes? It doesn't make sense. I'll keep doing what I've always done and get by."

William's issue is *I'm not safe* and *I can't trust anyone.* It's a double whammy that causes him to be Mr. Tough Guy. *If I can't trust the out-side world, then I better be ready to fight.* With a temperament like this, the most easily displayed emotion is anger, which compels him to push down all other emotional experiences. In this case, William doesn't feel safe sharing his feelings with people because he can't trust them. People with this combination tend to push others away, and the only way for someone to be in a relationship with a person like this is to be subservient, in which case he or she is treated with much generosity. They stuff their emotions so deeply beneath the surface that it is difficult for them to feel anything. Anger is an easy cover-up for this condition.

Stephanie

◆ Fifty-six-year-old Stephanie, a successful bodyworker, has a pile of unopened mail, unpaid bills, and unanswered e-mails to attend to.

Stephanie says, "The bills aren't getting paid. Paperwork is overwhelming. I can't stand to look at the piles. I just don't know how to do this. I have no idea what it takes to run a business. I feel so overwhelmed by it all."

Stephanie's issue is *I am unacceptable*. This comes out in her as the statement *I am a terrible person*. This causes her to be highly self-critical, even more so than someone with the issue *I'm not good enough*. She engages in behaviors that reinforce her low opinion of herself and downplay her accomplishments. By not paying her bills and returning calls in a timely fashion, she succeeds in creating situations that confirm or reinforce her erroneous core belief.

Keith

◆ Forty-year-old Keith, a self-employed executive headhunter, spends hours online surfing the Web and making occasional purchases.

Keith says, "My work is very taxing, and I really have to relax, so I surf the Internet and sometimes I don't have enough time left in the day to get my work done. I guess I'm just a slacker."

Keith's issue is also *I'm unacceptable*. He believes he doesn't have the skills to do his job and engages in distracting behavior that reinforces his self-proclaimed unacceptability. When activated, people with this issue have great difficulty believing anything good about themselves.

They have a tendency to fall into bouts of self-pity because their life is so terrible, and they can't get motivated to do anything because they will be horrible at it anyway.

Veronica

◆ Thirty-one-year-old Veronica, a yoga instructor, is at odds with her business partner over how to run the business.

Veronica says, "This relationship is too difficult. We're running a yoga center and my partner is always travelling. She's never here and expects me to do all the work, then judges me for not doing it right."

Veronica's issue is *I am not heard.* In her case, it is she who is not listening to herself. She projects this onto others and becomes defensive. By doing this, she distracts from her own inner voice and feels like she's a victim. She defends her position, especially when she receives supportive, critical feedback, and doesn't even consider the veracity of what someone else is saying. People with this issue activated may defend their position very loudly or may have difficulty finding his or her voice. Their defensiveness usually creates a reaction in the other person, resulting in an unfulfilling, unrewarding interaction.

Bethany

◆ Forty-seven-old Bethany, a manager of a health-food store, experiences discomfort around the owner of the store, who the employees agree behaves aggressively.

Bethany says, "If I stay out of sight when my boss is around, I won't have to deal with him."

Bethany's issue is *I'm not safe.* When activated, this issue causes her to see the world and people around her as threats. She perceives danger in places it does not exist and protects herself by withdrawing, as she does when her boss visits the store. There are certainly dangers in the world, but when someone has the issue *I'm not safe,* it is difficult for them to make a distinction between an actual threat and a perceived threat. This has the potential to negatively impact one's ability to take professional and personal risks.

People come in a variety of shapes and sizes with all different types of personalities, and even though the underlying issue may be the same from one person to the next, everyone will react to issue activation in a variety of ways. Also, certain situations can activate a different combination of issues. Some generalities can be made, but it is impossible to fit each person into a predetermined set of behaviors. It's important to allow room for variations and surprises in this world.

ISSUE ACTIVATION: PUSHING THE I-SPOT

When an issue is activated, you may or may not be aware that you are in *reaction* to a situation. You may think you are responding appropriately. This is because when you are in the thick of things, it's difficult to separate yourself from the explosive feelings you are experiencing. This is why the pause button is so handy (see page 20). Even if you are aware that our insidious virus has temporarily taken over your operating system, it may still be difficult to step back and see the situation objectively and remain balanced, flexible, and strong. As soon as an issue is activated, your ability to accurately and clearly experience a situation is diminished. While a minor issue activation will only moderately distort your ability to perceive a situation accurately, a major issue activation will completely affect the story that you create around a situation. An issue-activated story is bound to an erroneous core belief, and this prevents any possibility of drawing accurate conclusions about the events.

When the I-spot is pressed, it will usually generate predictable and recurring emotional reactions to events. These physical and emotional explosions prevent the mind from remaining neutral to the outside events that stimulated this inner reaction. Once issue activation

Veronica's Experience
OPPOSING VIEWPOINTS

Before Veronica began the program, she didn't know why she would become so defensive when confronted with an opposing viewpoint or an idea that didn't fit her belief system. She approached every agitating situation as an opportunity to prove that a person with an opposing viewpoint was wrong. She believed the other person's "erroneous" position on a topic could be changed if they just listened to what she had to say. She'd often heard herself saying, "Why isn't so-and-so listening to me?" If someone else was at fault, it gave her the perfect excuse to not look at her own issue or to listen to what was going on inside. She sincerely believed that she was responding appropriately to another person's imbalance instead of getting curious about her own emotional upset.

occurs, the mind creates a series of thoughts, or stories, that at best prevent us from being an impartial witness to events and at worst propel us into drawing conclusions and displaying behaviors that are both out of proportion and inappropriate to the situation. Everyone can recall at least a few cases in which they couldn't believe that they had such a strong reaction to a particular situation that normally wouldn't faze them.

Most negative or unwanted behaviors originate from issue activations. They prevent us from being fully present to the moment. Once activated, these issues confuse and distort the present moment, forcing us to struggle with the past. This compulsive reliving of the past is then projected onto the present situation, creating the illusion that the story in our mind about the present situation is accurate. The term "self-fulfilling prophecy" might be coming to mind right now.

Issue activation occurs when an erroneous core belief is reignited deep within the mind. There is typically only one issue that becomes active in a particular situation, but a few minor ones can interfere at the same time. It's important to know that issue activation occurs instantly. One moment you feel perfectly balanced, and the next moment something happens and you are instantly agitated. It is a slippery slope from balance to agitation. The nature of an erroneous core belief is that it is beneath the surface. It does not advertise itself to the conscious mind. Like a cat lurking in the shadows, it springs upon the mouse of our awareness without warning just when we are most vulnerable. For example, Cynthia is having a wonderful time with friends until she hears that a mutual acquaintance is getting married. Without warning, a trapdoor opens inside her heart and she plummets downward into a sea of regret and lost opportunities. Her belief that there is something wrong with her is activated at the most inopportune time. A wonderful dinner with friends becomes a battleground between her balanced, aware self and her issue-activated, insecure self that is crying out for love and attention. Cynthia has no control over the external catalysts in her life; she lives in constant dread of being reminded that "there is something wrong" with being a thirty-nine-year-old woman who is single and childless.

Mark's attempt to remain civil and relaxed while listening to his

ex-wife's complaints that his child support is far below what she believes is fair creates a perfect storm. His attempt to suppress his anger toward her is coupled with the injustice of having to pay for child support even when his daughter has spent the entire summer with him. Self-righteousness rears its ugly head as he argues that her hypocrisy is beyond limits. One moment he is in control and the next he slides down the dangerous slope of self-pity, blame, and anger.

The amount of awareness present is critical at the moment when everything inside of us is screaming negative aphorisms and forcing us to experience an emotion that we work very hard to suppress.

Although cause and effect seem to be the culprit, the actual situation, as you've learned, is innocent of causing the reaction. Events in our lives merely act as the catalyst to set inner issues in motion. The event activates a belief that results in a preprogrammed mental reaction. These reactions occur immediately, creating a story that will always to some degree misrepresent the truth of a situation.

Once we are aware of the erroneous belief we've been repeating to ourselves—subconsciously up until now—we are better prepared to observe the reaction, know the source of the disturbance, and eventually deactivate the issue. For now, it's important to recognize what we've been doing to temporarily distract from and suppress the issue.

REMAINING STRONG

The activation of an erroneous core belief is a powerful occurrence that can create emotional explosions that could easily throw us off balance and create tension and inflexibility. In order to remain aware during these upsetting moments, we need a great deal of fortitude and focus. We need to be strong enough to relax around the event, pause, and get back to center. Physical and mental strength is necessary to successfully remain aware during a situation driven by an issue activation.

DISTRACTING FROM AND SUPPRESSING THE ISSUE

When you are out of sync, when your issue has been activated and you are trying to turn off the issue activation (the I-spot), you will probably go to great lengths to make everything better so that you *feel* better. You may go about this in a multitude of ways, some of which may be harmful, such as eating fattening comfort food or indulging in alcohol or drugs. Others may not be harmful, such as going for a jog or sitting in meditation. Either way, there is something you are avoiding. As you'll learn in Chapter 4, the steps you take to "rectify the situation" are usually short-lived, and before you know it, your issue will be activated again. The cast of characters may be different, the setting may be different, but your feelings about the situation will be very familiar. You'll notice that you're stuck in a vicious cycle—which we call the Frustration Cycle.

> *At any given moment, there are three possibilities within you: (1) Everything is supporting harmony (there is zero percent issue activation and you are completely open to experience enlightening moments); (2) Some things are supporting harmony (there is less than 100 percent issue activation and the experience of enlightening moments is less likely but still possible); or (3) Nothing is supporting harmony (there is 100 percent issue activation and you are completely unavailable to experience enlightening moments).*

To illustrate how we distract and suppress, let's consider a few of the people we've been discussing throughout this chapter and the last. Although they were eventually able to resolve their relationship difficulties through employing the tools and taking the steps, let's look at the methods they used to temporarily make themselves feel better. Jason, for instance, spent a lot of time fantasizing about romance and writing poetry to distract from his issue, while Cynthia engaged in physically taxing sports and kept herself busy with work to distract herself from uncomfortable feelings. Stephanie, meanwhile, distracted herself with television and food. Notice that none of these distractions were harmful per se, but they were still distractions, because they were suppressing the emotional content that had been temporarily brought to the surface when their I-spot was pushed. There are myriad distractions, of course, and we'll examine them more closely in Chapter 4.

> *If we are unconscious of our reactions to situations, we cannot experience any growth. As human beings, we have the ability to be self-reflective. We can be aware of ourselves and how we operate. But if we choose to remain unaware by continuously engaging in distractions and suppressing uncomfortable feelings, we will continue to repeat the same mistakes over and over again.*

The important thing to note here is that it is the lack of awareness with which we do something that makes it a distraction. In other words, if you feel uncomfortable and engage in some activity or behavior to "feel better," then you can be sure that you are distracting yourself from the issue activation by remaining unaware.

Karen's Experience

IDENTIFYING HER ISSUE

 Karen, the CEO of a successful engineering firm, was having difficulty adjusting to life after her second divorce. This last divorce was particularly heartbreaking for her because she felt forced into it by her husband's infidelity. She was very angry, which was certainly understandable. However, even after a year had passed, Karen was still making negative, disparaging comments about her ex-husband to whomever would listen whenever she had the opportunity.

These negative comments fueled Karen's anger, and eventually, her complaints and rants became tiresome to her friends. A close friend of hers finally got up the courage to suggest to her that this was no longer about the ex-husband but about Karen herself and her inability (and unwillingness) to move on with life.

That's when Karen began the program. She learned that she needed to develop the willingness and strength to look within and discover what was going on for her beneath the surface. What she eventually discovered was that the anger she was perpetuating was a distraction from feeling the loneliness of being single once again. Her issue, *I am all alone,* was so painful for her to deal with directly that it took many sessions and much effort on her part to develop the fortitude and focus necessary to really sit with the sadness and loneliness. Part of her program was to engage in a mind-strengthening exercise so that she wouldn't be so susceptible to angry thoughts. Eventually, through practicing this and other exercises and doing the work, she was able to move past her anger and on with her life.

❧ Mind-Strengthening Exercise ❧

We use our minds all the time, but few of us have the strength of mind necessary to keep it focused on something uncomfortable without distracting ourselves from it. For many people, the mind is like a puppy who doesn't yet recognize its owner's commands. This particular exercise helps train the mind to stay on one point without leaving it until you give it the appropriate command. The power of concentration that comes with a focused mind increases our success in both our professional and personal lives. The benefits of a strong mind include an improved memory, better problem-solving skills, and greater clarity.

To perform this exercise, sit in a quiet place with your back straight and your head and neck in a supported, comfortable position. Begin the three-part breathing you learned in the Breathing for Awareness Exercise in Chapter 1 (see page 30) until you experience a state of ease and relaxation throughout your entire body. Once you have achieved that goal, allow your breath to move on its own without any attention to counting the inhalations or exhalations. Now, observe the movement of your breath, literally imagining that you are sitting in a movie theater watching an enjoyable movie of your lungs expanding as the air moves into them as you inhale and then deflating as the air exits them as you exhale.

After you have watched this movie for a time and you are feeling even more relaxed, begin counting each inhalation and exhalation as a single repetition. Keep focused, concentrating on each repetition. If you are interrupted by a thought, sound, or smell (literally anything that distracts you or takes your attention away from counting each breath), go back to *one* and start counting all over again. When your mind wanders, be sure to start back at one. The objective of this exercise is to see how high your count goes before you become distracted. Do this for five minutes at a time with the intention of increasing your count each time you practice. Record the results in your journal so you can keep track of your progress. If you master five minutes, go to ten, then fifteen, and so on until your focus is very strong.

🕸 *Experience for the Road* 🕸

Pay very close attention to your reactions (as opposed to your responses) to events that take place. Remind yourself to be aware by posting notes around the house. When your internal alarm goes off indicating that something has pressed your I-spot, be strong and stay present in the moment. Do whatever you can to stay alert so that you can examine with awareness what's going on for you. Be fully present to your frustration, anger, disappointment, or any other subtle or not-so-subtle issue activations. Rate your issue activations on a scale of mild, medium, or intense. Be particularly sensitive to the stories in your mind. Journal about the situation, the story, and the issue. Also journal about specifics such as how, when, where, and why your issue got activated. Be aware of how often you experience an issue activation and how long it lasts before you distract from it. Do not judge yourself when doing this exercise. Simply be an observer.

Separating the story from the situation and identifying the issue take earnest practice. When you pay close attention to these factors, the patterns in your behavior and your reactions to situations are going to begin revealing themselves. When your patterns reveal themselves, they shed light on your thoughts and reactions, inviting you to see them from a fresh perspective. Having more clarity regarding how you operate is the first step in understanding the power of the Frustration Cycle, which we will tackle next.

CHAPTER 4

The Frustration Cycle
Recognizing the Patterns

*Insanity is doing the same thing over and over again
and expecting a different result.*
—ATTRIBUTED TO ALBERT EINSTEIN

When we are feeling stuck in some area of our life, or when one or more of our relationships is unsatisfactory, or when we feel that there's something more waiting right around the corner but we just don't have any forward momentum, we are caught in the Frustration Cycle. Many of us are. In fact, it's part of human nature. Most people—especially those who have not begun this journey—are completely oblivious to the fact that they are caught in this continuous loop of dissatisfaction and dis-ease. They keep making the same mistakes, ending up in the same type of situations, feeling those same uncomfortable feelings after interacting with a particular person (or type of person) or a specific event. But now you are one step ahead. You are aware that something isn't quite right, and knowing that you are in the Frustration Cycle gives you the clear message that something needs to change. In this chapter, you'll use what you've learned in the previous three chapters to start identifying your patterns: the recurring situations in your life, your reactions to them, and how you distract yourself from them rather than

working through them. A huge shift of awareness occurs as you begin
to observe previously unconscious behaviors and reactions by recognizing that there are other options available. It is only through iden-
tification with your patterns that you can begin to break them down
into their component parts and rearrange them to make a new pattern that's more in tune with your objectives. Let's begin by taking a
look at a graphic representation of the Frustration Cycle (Figure 4.1).
When we are caught in its loop, we are experiencing the same patterns over and over again.

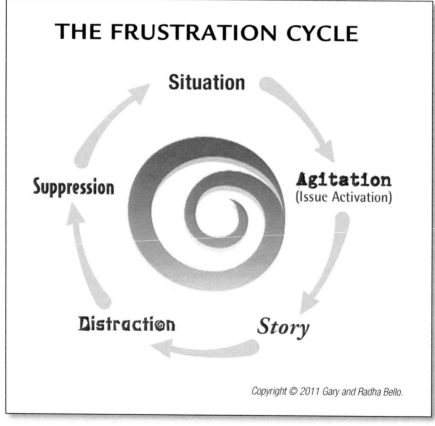

Figure 4.1. The Frustration Cycle. This is a graphic representation of the circular
pattern we engage in when we avoid dealing with our issues directly.

Nelson's Experience
THE NEVER-ENDING CYCLE

Nelson was a relatively young widower with children who was ready to seek out a new life partner, but none of the women he dated seemed to meet his expectations of a wife and mother. He'd often discount someone on the first date by identifying a quality or characteristic about her that he found unacceptable. His date would say or do something or look at him a certain way, and he would decide on the spot that a relationship with her wouldn't work. He would then get that sinking feeling that he and the kids would be alone forever—the recurring agitation that frustrated him to no end—and the date would be doomed.

Nelson's situation was simply that he was looking for a mate and a female role model for his children. His story was that no woman could meet his expectations. Needless to say, Nelson's situation was a never-ending cycle of searching for the perfect woman for him and being disappointed that no one he dated could meet his expectations. This was his pattern. Recognizing this pattern and truly desiring to change it was his first step in getting out of this unwanted groove.

EXAMINING SITUATIONAL PATTERNS
AND RECURRING AGITATION

While you are becoming more aware, you will not only notice that there are patterns to the situations that occur in your life, but you will be starting to recognize them as they occur. Part of Nelson's pattern (see above) was to look for some flaw in his date the very first time they got together, and he would then use this as an excuse to not get

together with her a second time. His dating experiences became very predictable. Knowing this, the next time he was on a date and found himself focusing on something he didn't like about his date, he noted that he was falling into the same old routine and focused instead on the conversation.

George, the board president we discussed in Chapters 2 and 3, made excellent decisions in business and knew how to use the expertise of his employees. In his personal life, however, his decision-making abilities were based on avoiding uncomfortable situations, which resulted in making poor decisions. When faced with a problem in his personal life, he would try to make it go away in the easiest fashion possible—even if it meant going against his intuition—because it didn't operate like a business. For instance, when friends approached him for financial assistance, even when he knew it was not in the best interest of either the person or himself, he would still acquiesce. When he became curious, he began to see why he was not following his intuition in personal matters; he realized that his pattern of giving in to avoid discomfort was not beneficial for anyone involved. It was essential for him to notice and overcome his discomfort in having to say no to a friend or loved one.

Jason, who we also discussed in Chapters 2 and 3, would talk to his girlfriend about his deep feelings for her and then wait for a response. She would feel uncomfortable with this raw emotion and would remain silent. Jason would then go off to sulk and write poetry to make himself feel better. Feeling better, he would share the love poetry with his girlfriend (which was essentially the same thing as talking to her about his feelings), and again, she would not respond. What seemed like two different scenarios really arose from the same pattern. Jason was finally able to see how this pattern wasn't serving him. Eventually he broke up with this woman because he realized this situation wasn't working for either of them. He also recognized this pattern when it began to occur in his next relationship and was able to respond differently.

Finally, in Bethany's case, whenever she was faced with confrontation, her pattern was to withdraw from the situation. For example, when her boss came into the store, she would find busywork to do in the office so that she wouldn't have to interact with him. This pattern also appeared in other areas of her life. She'd been overbilled for a hospital stay, and because it required that she stand up for herself, she avoided taking the necessary steps, again withdrawing from the situation. Once she realized that her pattern was to withdraw, she worked on developing alternative strategies.

What are the recurring patterns in your life that aren't working for you? Do you find yourself withdrawing from people or experiences and then find yourself complaining that no one includes you? Do you find yourself sitting in front of the television eating mindlessly and then complain that you are gaining weight? Do you fail to express your opinion and then complain that no one listens to you? Are you dating people who are consistently emotionally unavailable or incompatible with you? Do you find that you distract yourself by going for a walk in nature when you get upset rather than staying present and confronting the issue? Do your friends and acquaintances take advantage of your good nature? Do you fight with your siblings whenever you are together? Do you find a glass of wine or two to be a soothing necessity at the end of a difficult day? Do you wake up in the middle of the night ruminating about an agitating situation and often find that you're unable to get back to sleep? Do you shrink every time you speak to one of your parents? Are you in a dead-end job that you hate but tolerate? Do you keep getting passed over for promotions? Do you find yourself saying things you didn't mean when something is not going your way? Do you allow people to speak to you in a less than kind way? Is your temper inappropriate in certain situations? Do you have difficulty expressing yourself in groups? Are you afraid to try new things and constantly limit yourself to certain experiences because of fear? If your answer is yes to any of these or similar questions, you are stuck in an unproductive pattern—or even more than one.

Situational patterns also cause patterns of agitation. Agitation can manifest physically, mentally, and emotionally—as a physical sensation, as a recurring thought, and an emotional upset. For example, after having a debate with his father, Leo would stew in his anger and replay the heated conversation over and over in his mind, despite not wanting to think about it. His jaw would begin to hurt from clenching it so tightly. More often than not, Leo would feel this way after an interaction with his father, even though he had planned for a better outcome before the conversation occurred. Lisa had a similar problem with her subordinate at work. She would ask him to handle a certain task in a certain way, and he would argue that he had a better way to do it. Then, she would become angry thinking that her authority was being questioned and insist he do it her way. Her shoulders would become very stiff, and her breath would become short. She was appalled by his arrogance every time this happened. In Leo's case, he blamed his father, and in Lisa's case, she blamed her subordinate for the agitated feelings. Both Leo and Lisa felt that if only the other person would change his position and be more responsible, they would feel better.

It is not always going to be an interaction with another person that results in your feeling agitated in a familiar way. Perhaps you tense up every time you are faced with paying your bills and a feeling of dread overcomes you. Or you read the paper and become incensed over some injustice in the world and "see red." Or possibly when driving, you are appalled that people drive so recklessly while texting.

When you directly address the agitation you are feeling, rather than trying to change or control the situation, you'll see that the agitation you are feeling is the actual culprit and the part you can change, and you will no longer feel victimized by the situation. Of course,

FEELING VICTIMIZED

There is a world of difference between feeling victimized by everyday situations such as getting passed over for a promotion or thinking that no one understands your point of view and being a victim of abuse or violence. These are separate issues that go beyond the scope of this book. If you are, or have been, a victim of abuse or violence, we advise you to seek the counsel of a trained professional.

Moreover, abuse suffered as a child often results in at least some self-blame, arising in thoughts such as *What have I done to deserve this? Why am I so unlovable? Why am I being punished?* and *Nothing that I do is good enough.* Thoughts such as these often become buried deep inside along with the feelings experienced during the abuse. The process of healing involves many of the strategies mentioned in this book, but because the memories and feelings can be so intense, a good therapist can help make the healing process safer and faster.

Similarly, adults can face violence, abuse, loss, and tragedy as well. Recovery from such pain can take time, and we therefore need to try to be patient and self-compassionate. Once again, it may be useful to reach out for help and support during very challenging and painful times.

you'll have some work ahead of you regarding the agitation itself, but at least you'll be able to put an end to the victim mentality that keeps you continuously rehashing the circumstances in your mind and acting them out in your life again and again.

SEEING THE PATTERNS IN THE STORIES

In Chapter 2, you learned that there are many different types of stories we tell ourselves about the situations that occur in our lives. These stories arise from our feelings regarding the situation, and sometimes they are accurate, but quite often they are corrupted by the virus in our operating system. When our I-spot is pressed, suddenly we cannot perceive things clearly because our vision has become clouded—the light of awareness is blotted out, and the path ahead becomes fuzzy. Our perceptions are now skewed, and we are unable to be objective.

Situation $\longrightarrow$ Agitation $\longrightarrow$ Corrupted Story $\longrightarrow$
Inability to Perceive the Situation Accurately

We usually think our story is accurately based on the facts of the situation, but quite often, it is just some variation of a recurring theme: specifically, a theme in which we are somehow a victim. Take Michael, for example. As you may recall, Michael had difficulty with employee retention. Each of his research assistants gave him a different reason for leaving, so he felt justified in blaming them for deserting him. In actuality, it was his inability to treat his employees with dignity and respect that caused them to quit. The same thing happened with his ex-wife. After many years of feeling like she was being treated unfairly, she asked for a divorce. Again, he blamed her for not sticking around. Whether or not Michael could see it at the time, this was a perfect example of two different situations resulting in the same type of a corrupted story, thus re-creating the same pattern. A less extreme example of this is someone who is consistently late always blaming the traffic and other outside circumstances for their tardiness when in actuality they just need to give themselves more time to get where they're going. Rather than take responsibility for having a pattern of being late, their story involves the incompetency of other drivers and the circumstances of traffic. In another case, someone who is consistently passed over for a promotion may create a story that blames failure to achieve on the boss's preference for a certain type of person when, in fact, he or she is simply not performing up to the boss's standards. Again, rather than take responsibility, this person blames someone else for his or her own shortcomings rather than working on the areas in which he or she may be lacking. And last, consider the person who always falls back on the story about how his or her parents failed to do such and such or did such and such when they were growing up, and therefore any shortcomings they have are their parents' fault.

When you finally begin to take notice of the repetition in the stories you tell yourself, you'll become bored by them. You've got the same story repeating itself over and over again, and it's almost like watching the same old television reruns. It's time to change the channel. You're ready to get to the heart of the matter and ask yourself, *Deep down inside of me, what is causing my reaction?* This is an essential question. You need to know what the issue is. You need to know what is happening inside of you that is distorting the facts and making you feel so uncomfortable and disconnected from your true wisdom and intuition. Take another look at the erroneous core beliefs (see page 66) and *feel* your reaction to the statements so you can begin to recognize what's going on in your subconscious mind.

It's also important to note that we develop a certain attachment to our stories, which is why we keep returning to similar types of stories. This is because they are sometimes connected to memories that may have been upsetting and are still unresolved. As long as a trauma is unhealed, it continues to influence our stories. We become so identified with our stories that they seem accurate, and we do not realize that if we really paid close attention, we could stop telling them. As long as the old stories continue to assist us in not taking responsibility for our issue(s), we will naturally remain attached to them.

Mark, the lieutenant colonel in the army discussed earlier, had the same story again and again: *I'm always the one who has to be the bigger person. I always have to be aware and compensate for other people's inadequacies. Why does it always have to be me who says I'm sorry?* What Mark is really saying is *Why isn't anyone there for me?* He doesn't see this, of course, because he is attached to the story that he is always there for others, but others are not there for him.

This particular pattern of stories results in Mark feeling resentment toward his ex-wives or himself, which further deepens his loneliness. His resentment is a desperate attempt to cover up the issue—in other words, to distract himself from agitation. For Mark, the trauma that keeps his story alive is the times in his life when he had been abandoned, either real or imagined.

It is important to start noticing the flavor and texture of your patterned stories. Notice how they affect your energy. Notice if they are uplifting or deflating. Also, start paying more attention to how your stories are received by others. Do people give you the impression that they've heard it all before? Pay attention also to the physical sensations you have when you are telling your stories. Do you become short of breath? Does your face get hot? Do you tense up? Does your stomach begin to quiver? You will begin to notice these physical patterns as well. Anything you do to increase your awareness and give you some distance from your stories will help you to start recognizing the patterns, thereby giving you the opportunity to change them.

UNCOVERING THE PATTERNS TO DISTRACTIONS

A distraction is something that diverts our attention away from something else. It is an obstacle to concentration. There are various forms of distraction. Not all of them will be what you might consider a distraction, such as drinking alcohol, smoking cigarettes, or overeating. We all know that such distractions can be detrimental to our physical health, but distractions can also be healthy activities, such as going for a brisk walk, meditating, or reading a quality piece of literature. However, distractions don't always fall neatly into the positive/negative categories. The things we do every day or very often, such as working, healthy eating, texting, talking on the phone, having sex, shopping, meditating, religious observances, socializing, and so on, can also become distractions when we are doing them to avoid feeling the agitation we are experiencing in reaction to something. Distractions can even be the very stories we tell ourselves. We get so caught up in all our stories that we distract ourselves from the core feelings that

NOTICING A LACK OF BALANCE?

Quite often, when an aspect of your life seems out of balance with others—for example, you are working too much and not exercising enough, or you are spending too much time on the Internet and not spending enough time with your family—that is a good indication that you are distracting in a pretty big way. It is usually a pattern that is so ingrained and familiar to you that it almost feels normal, but you know deep down that you would benefit from having a more balanced lifestyle. And, sometimes, you may actually distract with things that literally throw you and your body off-kilter.

Knowing how important balance is to this inner work, it's essential that you take the time to examine what parts of your life are a bit askew and what you may be doing to further impede your inner equilibrium. Once you recognize the imbalance that is characteristic of some of your patterns, you can begin to take steps to make healthier choices and forge new patterns that will bring balance to all aspects of your life.

caused the agitation in the first place. And last, but not least, emotions themselves, such as anger and fear, can also be powerful distractions.

So, it's not exactly *what* you are doing that makes something a distraction but rather the intention with which you are doing it. This is an important distinction: If you are engaging in a healthy activity such as meditation simply for the enjoyment of it or for the opportunities for growth it offers, or if you are engaging in the activity to increase your awareness, clear your mind, and freshen your perspective, then you are not using it as a distraction. However, if you are meditating to avoid feeling an emotion, then you are certainly using it as a distraction. Here's an extreme example: An entire community of meditators were being taught that when they became upset they should avoid interactions with the individual or situation and immediately go meditate. Although this sounds lofty and spiritual, the truth was that the entire community was being taught to avoid sharing their feelings and dealing with various dysfunctional behaviors. Instead of being truthful and honest, many of them would retreat to their rooms hoping to find peace. This type of peace is only momentary when it is being used to cover over uncomfortable emotions that result from real situations requiring attention.

What do you do to soothe your agitation when it comes up? What are the patterns to your distractions? Are they healthy or unhealthy? Do your distractions require activity or inactivity? Cynthia, the successful entrepreneur we discussed in Chapters 2 and 3, found her distraction in skiing. Whenever she was feeling agitated, upset, or overwhelmed, she would take an unscheduled trip to go skiing. It wasn't until she realized that even something as refreshing as skiing could be used to suppress uninvited emotional turmoil that she began to look at dealing with the issue more directly.

Not everyone can go skiing to distract themselves, of course, so some people use more mundane distractions such as watching television or jogging. There are smaller momentary distractions too, such as bouncing one's legs, fingernail biting, wringing hands, cracking knuckles, and so on. Other people might engage in obviously destructive distractions such as smoking. When it comes to smoking, the patterns are easy to recognize since it is such a ritualistic practice. However, whatever the distraction is, if we look closely enough, we will uncover the pattern. For example, *I'm biting my nails. What just happened?* A person who examines this may realize that an uncomfortable thought had just entered his or her mind and suddenly that hangnail needed attention! That's an easy one. Other patterns may not be so obvious. The list of distractions that people use could go on and on, but there will always be a pattern when we look closely enough.

When we engage in a distraction to avoid feeling the emotions associated with our agitation, we are putting another layer between ourselves and our feelings. Regardless of *how* we are doing it, when we are stuck in the Frustration Cycle, we are not processing our agitation.

WHAT WE HAVE LEARNED ABOUT ATTACHMENT TO OUR PATTERNS

Thinking about objects will attach you to them;
Grow attached, and you become addicted;
Thwart your addiction, it turns to anger;
Be angry, and you confuse your mind;
Confuse your mind, you forget the lesson of experience;
Forget experience, you lose discrimination;
Lose discrimination, and you miss life's only purpose.
—BHAGAVAD GITA

Many years ago, Radha and I took a trip around the world. We realized almost right away that living outside our cultural comfort zone would give us many opportunities to become more aware of our patterns. When we made our first stop in England, although certainly a different world than the one we'd been living in, the pattern of living was only slightly different, so there was no huge discomfort. However, by the time we had traveled through Europe, Greece, and Turkey, the gradual shift to experiencing a completely different lifestyle and way of thinking pushed us out of our comfort zone. We became acutely aware of how attached we were to Western comforts as we passed through Afghanistan, Pakistan, India, Sri Lanka, Thailand, and Indonesia.

Having said that, we were pleased to discover that the changes in our lifestyle had many rewarding side effects. Besides giving us a tremendous opportunity to change such areas as diet, communication, exercise, and the difference in how different cultures communicate, we totally loved the freedom of living outside our established patterns. It was delightful to live without being in control and seeing the benefits of remaining curious to all the unknowns that presented themselves at every turn in the road.

Almost weekly, as we moved on to another location, our favorite dishes had to fall by the wayside, making room for a new and completely unknown culinary delight (or not). That is where we noticed how quickly the mind becomes accustomed to objects once experienced. The first time is a completely unknown experience, the second time (if a dish tastes really good, for instance) is no longer a new experience, but there is attachment to having it again, and if there is a third time, it meant we *really* liked that dish and a pattern was established; our taste buds hungered for that taste to be repeated.

Patterns or tendencies are the way the mind deals with past experiences. If the interaction with a person, place, or thing is enjoyable, or if it supports the direction we are taking in our life, it soon becomes a pattern. Now comes the important part of this process as mentioned in the Gita quote: "Grow attached, and you become addicted." As silly as this may sound, consider what would happen if you became attached to your chair. Everywhere you went, the chair would hinder your movement, though when you needed to rest, it would certainly be useful.

Having attachments causes us to lose our freedom. If we carry erroneous core beliefs (the unconscious attachment to something that is not true), they decrease our awareness and limit our ability to be available to all the unknowns in our lives. Patterns can be useful or not; attachments can be healthy or unhealthy. However, if we become too attached, problems arise. When an attachment turns into a desire, a problem begins to develop. How do you know if a pattern has turned into a desire? Just take it away or prevent yourself from experiencing it.

Many times, my clients' immediate and incredulous reaction to a suggestion that they refrain from a particular behavior or an unhealthy food indicates that their attachment has turned to desire. And when a desire is thwarted, causing an agitated reaction, we can be certain that an addiction is lurking below the surface. Radha and I have often heard addictions described as a devotion to something that is harmful to us, and that supports the findings from our work.

Addiction can also be viewed as a *method of distraction*. If William's lunch includes a couple of beers, and he returns to work feeling less agitated, this could be the beginning of an unhealthy pattern. As a matter of fact, once he became aware of that negative pattern, he was able to switch over to his relaxation and breathing exercises to calm his jumbled nerves.

Addiction is a serious physical and mental disturbance that needs professional care and supervision. Our programs are not designed as a replacement for addiction therapy and counseling. It is our experience that there are no shortcuts for dealing with serious addictive behavior, and because of that, we refer clients to a network of health professionals. However, for those whose patterns include unhealthy choices that mask an underlying issue, our program will increase your awareness to a level that allows you to make the appropriate changes.

SUPPRESSING THE ISSUE

Once you've engaged in your distraction long enough, and it has succeeded in squashing or numbing your feelings, you have reached the eleven o'clock position in the Frustration Cycle. All seems well for now, but when the clock strikes midnight (the situation or some variation of the situation occurs again), you are bound to repeat the same old actions and feel the same old upset and frustration. You haven't made any progress.

You haven't made any progress because suppressing an issue is analogous to holding a beach ball underwater. Imagine it's a beautiful day, nice and hot, and you're in the community pool having a good time. Then, someone comes along and says, "I'll give you a million dollars if you can hold this beach ball underwater for twenty-four hours. No part of the ball can be allowed to break the surface of the water."

You look at the ball. It's a *big* beach ball. It's nice and hard. It's fully inflated. *A million dollars?* "Well, all right. I'll do it," you say. If you have any experience trying to keep a beach ball underwater for any length of time, you know this is one difficult task. It's going to take a *tremendous* amount of energy and constant effort. Once you've succeeded in pushing it as far under the water as you can, you get by for a while by sitting on it, and maybe you'll even forget that you're holding it down, but eventually, you *are* going to get tired, or someone is going to come along and distract you, or maybe you'll get splashed in the face—whatever the case may be, that beach ball is going to make its way to the surface, and you will not get that million dollars. Perhaps if you had deflated the beach ball—in other words, dealt directly with the agitation—you wouldn't have missed out on this fortune. Whatever the case may be, suppression only provides temporary relief. A new situation will always arise, which in turn will lead to the same patterns of agitation.

A RECAP OF THE FRUSTRATION CYCLE

How does the Frustration Cycle begin? A situation occurs. Situations occur all the time, of course, but not all of them result in feelings of frustration. No, this situation occurs and you immediately experience some kind of emotional explosion. An issue has been activated. You feel agitation. There is a powerful, uncomfortable feeling at play. Your I-spot has been pushed. Almost immediately you begin thinking and analyzing—in other words, creating stories to validate your feelings or to talk yourself out of them. Where does the material for your story come from? From the issue activation and the situation. So most likely, your story is going to have some parts of the situation (the facts), but it's also going to be powered, fueled, and energized by an erroneous core belief.

Let's take a look at an example. The phone rings and you look at the caller ID (the situation). When you see who it is, you tense up and feel upset (an issue is activated). *I don't want to answer the phone; she is just going to push my buttons and upset me,* you tell yourself (the story). Using that example, what's next in this cycle? Distraction. You decide not to answer the phone. You press the little button on your cell phone and it goes to voice mail. A few moments later, in order to thoroughly suppress your agitation, you have a glass of wine or listen to some relaxing music. Obviously, one of these distractions is a healthier choice than the other, but that's not the concern here. The key here is to link the distraction to the issue activation. That's what's important in this cycle. It's important because the distraction, healthy or unhealthy, is the problem. The distraction allows you to suppress the issue, and once the issue is suppressed, it will not surface again until the next situation—or when you look down at your phone and see that the person you didn't want to talk to left you a voice mail. Uh-oh! You tense up and feel upset. You decide to have another glass of wine or go for a walk and ignore the message for now. . . .

SITUATIONS ARE CATALYSTS

Although it's probably quite certain to you at this point in the book that situations are innocuous events that happen around us, they do affect us internally on a mental, emotional, and physical level. They activate our internal programming and we must interact in some way. We are in relationship with everything that touches our lives, and we have to function in some manner. When a situation pushes our button, our I-spot, our awareness of it provides us with an incredible opportunity to learn from the resulting agitation. In fact, the situations and people we encounter throughout our lives can reveal a tremendous amount of information about our personal inner workings, past actions, and present intentions. If we look closely, we can see those things reflected back at us on a daily basis, in the same way we see our reflection in a mirror. If you approach your day like an "adventure" lived through the looking glass—that is, recognize that everything that happens around you and every encounter you have is a direct result of your actions, past and present—your awareness will shift quite dramatically. People and circumstances that result in emotional discomfort or agitation are merely reflecting back at you those things about yourself that you don't feel comfortable with. On a subconscious level, we tend to be drawn to those people who best reflect our own shortcomings back at us, so that we have (on some level) the chance to rectify them in ourselves. This might sound counterintuitive; however, like much of what goes on subconsciously, it doesn't have to make sense. These are valuable lessons from the looking glass. We can choose to learn from the

> We're not quite there yet, but the goal is that every time we're upset, whenever these explosions occur within us, we want to become immediately aware of what's happening, know how to deactivate the true cause of the upset, bring ourselves back into balance, and be able to respond rather than react to the event.

lessons presented to us or we can try to avoid them. Recognizing your displeasure over the reflection you are seeing (in other words, knowing that something is amiss inside you) gives you the opportunity to pause, take action, reset your intentions, and make important changes.

Unfortunately, people tend to cover up the looking glass because they don't like what they see. That is akin to covering a mirror with a blanket because you have dirt on your face. Covering up the mirror is not going to make your face clean. It needs to be washed. Here's an example: If you have an interaction with someone and you feel the heat of anger suddenly rising over something you heard, this is the perfect opportunity to look a little closer from within and really examine what is causing your anger. Has the person questioned your integrity, insulted you, threatened you, taken advantage of you, or done or said something that caused an alarm to go off within you? What if it was a small child who called you poopy head? Would that make you angry? Probably not. You know you're not a poopy head.

You may tell the child that it's not nice to call people names, but that's just a lesson the child needs to learn. The child is not reflecting back at you what you might think of yourself. But what if some adult in either your professional or personal life tells you that you don't know what you're talking about? If that happens, an alarm goes off—an emotional explosion, or agitation. *They don't know what they are talking about,* your mind screams, and you have a reaction. This is a perfect signal to look more closely at yourself. Some part of you thinks the other person may be right or you wouldn't be so upset. That's the part of you that you need to address and not distract from or suppress.

William's Experience
OVERINDULGING TO DISTRACT

William is a "tough guy." Whenever a situation occurred in his life that elicited emotions outside of this tough-guy persona, such as sadness, sentimentality, or vulnerability, William's issue would become activated: *I can't trust anyone; it's not safe to show my feelings.* He would become agitated and would immediately withdraw emotionally and distract himself with destructive habits that would throw his body out of balance, such as overeating unhealthy foods, overindulging in alcohol, or participating in physically demanding activities that were too hard on his body. The only emotions he felt comfortable showing were anger and distrust.

William eventually developed high blood pressure and was placed on medication. He was only fifty and had damaged his body in many ways, and he didn't realize he could reverse some of the damage by switching over to healthy activities. He had engaged in this unbalanced, damaging cycle for so long that he didn't know he was in one. Part of William's work involved learning to be kinder to his body through a more balanced diet and less damaging exercise. In this way, his cycle could be interrupted, and through being kinder to his body he found that he could give himself an occasional break from being the tough guy. It would take some work, but William would eventually find his way off the medication and learn to process his feelings a little more freely. One of his early practices in this process was the exercise described below, which helped him find the balance he had been lacking not only in his body, but in his life. With this newfound equilibrium, he was able to tackle his issue directly without distracting.

❧ Pausing for Balance Exercise ❧

As you move forward with the lessons you are learning in this book, it is essential to continue to practice the Breathing for Awareness Exercise on page 30 as often as possible. Being aware of how you normally breathe makes it possible for you to be more acutely aware when you get out of balance. A change in your breathing is an early warning sign, an alarm, that something is churning inside you.

Our breath immediately reacts to emotional disturbances. It becomes irregular and shallow, thus creating an increased amount of carbon dioxide and acidity in the body, sending us into a state of imbalance. The high levels of acidity in the blood trigger the fight-or-flight reaction in the brain, which can easily result in an imbalanced reaction to an agitating event.

Once you have become adept at the Breathing for Awareness Exercise, you will want to employ it as soon as you recognize that your breathing has changed, indicating that you are upset. Immediately pause from any compulsion or need to deal with the situation and give yourself the opportunity to regain your equilibrium through your breath.

As you begin to practice the Breathing for Awareness Exercise during this pause in the action, pay very close attention to lengthening your exhalation to rid your body of excess carbon dioxide. As you breathe, count the number of repetitions it takes for you to return to a calm and balanced mental, emotional, and physical condition. (One repetition equals a deep inhalation and a long, slow exhalation.)

In your journal, record the number of breaths it took for you to return to a balanced state. Most likely, the more upset you are, the longer it will take. In any event, the object of this exercise is to eventually be able to get back into balance within three deep breaths. This will make it possible to pause for balance no matter where you are without anyone being the wiser!

❧ Experience for the Road ❦

For one week, at the end of every day, list each point of the Frustration Cycle in your journal. Next, think honestly about the events of the day, the emotions you felt, the reactions you had, the stories that you told yourself, the distractions you used, and whether or not you successfully suppressed the issue. Now, choose one of those situations and write your findings beside each point in the cycle. This will take some detective work because you are only just now bringing awareness to your patterns. Be sure to do this every day for at least a week and whenever you want to shed light on some day's events and your reaction to them. You might not know yet what the issue activation was for you, so look again at the list of erroneous core beliefs on pages 66 and 68–69 and pick the one that resonates with you in this particular instance. On the following page is a sample journey entry to help you on your way with this Experience for the Road activity.

JOURNAL ENTRY

Situation: Had conflict with coworker about the correct way to proceed with a project.

Issue Activation: *No one's listening to me.*

Story: She has no idea what she's talking about. She isn't making any sense. I wish she'd just listen to me long enough to understand what I'm saying. The whole project is going to get screwed up.

Distraction: Anger, resentment, argument; later, went to a movie and ate big tub of popcorn.

Suppression: For a while, still angry and agitated, especially after doing this exercise.

Additional Notes: The distraction worked until I started thinking about it again for this exercise. This must have reactivated the issue.

You are now familiar with how the Frustration Cycle operates in theory and hopefully in your daily life. You are probably also more aware—perhaps uncomfortably so—that it is you and you alone who keeps the cycle going through your reactions to the situations that occur in your life. Are you thinking of throwing the blanket over the mirror? Are you getting dizzy? Are you ready to hop off the wheel? Don't worry, you won't have to jump and roll. There is a "graceful" way out of the Frustration Cycle. And the good news is if you miss one exit, there will be many more opportunities.

CHAPTER 5

GRACE
Exiting the Frustration Cycle

We always look forward to the next time we're agitated.
It's an indication that there's a valuable lesson to be
learned and we have another exciting opportunity for growth.
—GARY AND RADHA

Now that you are familiar with the Frustration Cycle, as soon as you start to feel agitated in reaction to a situation, you're going to know that something is happening on a very deep level. You will instinctively know that you are no longer perceiving the situation clearly and that the story you're creating in your mind is corrupted by your issue, the erroneous core belief, the virus in your operating system. That virus is now determining what happens next. With all the training you've been through in the previous four chapters, you know that you are responsible for your reactions: you do not have to play the victim and get caught up in the Frustration Cycle again and again. No, you can put the Frustration Cycle to work for you as many of our clients have done. Along with the knowledge of your habitual patterns, you'll also be able to clearly identify when you have resorted to your old standby stories and distractions. This information gives you the opportunity to employ GRACE, an acronym for the five-step process for exiting the Frustration Cycle. The big question is, how exactly does one exit the Frustration Cycle? There's only one way: you *deactivate* the issue. Read on and get ready to exit the not-so-merry-go-round of frustration. (Turn to Appendix A for our clients' examples of working through GRACE.)

PUTTING THE FRUSTRATION CYCLE TO WORK FOR YOU

While you are learning and practicing this program, issue activations will be plentiful. Expect them and be gentle with yourself. If you once again find yourself cycling around frustration, remember to pause and breathe. Use every issue activation as an opportunity to practice exiting the cycle.

We have all been caught in the loop of the Frustration Cycle countless times throughout our lives. Operating without enough awareness keeps us spinning around this cycle again and again. However, now that we are aware when we are on this merry-go-round, we are ready to learn how to hop off. All this effort at becoming aware of our Frustration Cycle lights up the exit signs at any point in the loop. Take a look at the graphic representation of exiting the Frustration Cycle on the next page.

You can employ GRACE at any one of these exit points, but of course the earlier in the cycle you exit, the better off you'll be. Additionally, the more often you exit the Frustration Cycle through GRACE, the more skilled you will become at doing so. It just takes five easy-to-remember steps. We won't say they're easy steps, though. As with everything that ultimately benefits us, this will take some work. Chances are, when you're ready for step one, you are already on your way.

STEP ONE: GETTING AGITATED WITH AWARENESS

As human beings, it's perfectly natural for us to experience agitation in reaction to certain situations. It's going to happen. Expect it. Look

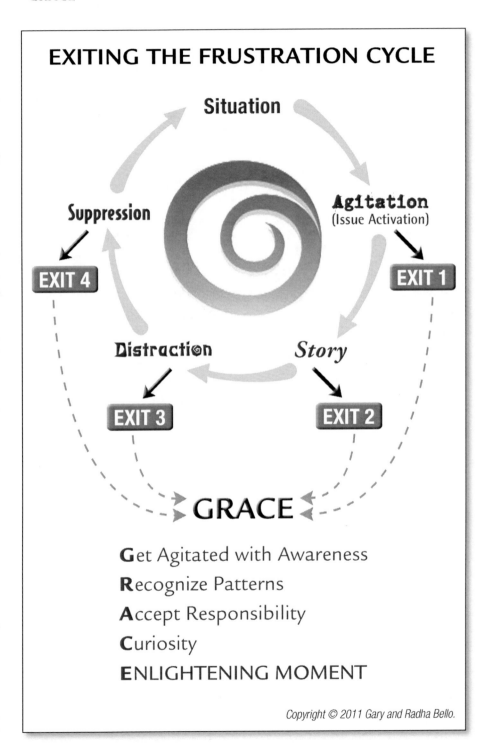

How Sweet the Sound

The acronym GRACE was directly inspired by Radha's mother, Gracie. A kind and loving woman, Gracie fully embodied the meaning of the word. She quickly deactivated her upsets with ease and was able to respond to people and events with a clear head and good intentions. The word *grace* amazingly represented the five-step process we had developed, each letter leading the way and setting forth a clear direction.

forward to it as an opportunity to grow. That's why the first step in GRACE, the "G," is to *get agitated with awareness*. In other words, feel it and examine it. Tell yourself, *I am aware of the agitation.* The sooner you are able to do this, the better off you'll be. The deeper you go without acknowledging the agitation, the more foggy and distorted your situation and story will become. You will grow more attached to your thoughts, and your perspective will be out of focus.

When you become aware of your agitation, you have accomplished the first step. The more aware you are, the less likely you will feel the need to distract yourself and get caught in the Frustration Cycle yet again. Of course, as with almost everything in life, this is easier said than done. As you've learned throughout this book, when we become agitated—when our issue is activated—our perception becomes cloudy and our awareness is compromised. You might not even be willing to acknowledge your agitation. This is where your balance, strength, and flexibility skills come in handy. When you practice being balanced physically, mentally, and emotionally, you'll instinctively know when you are off-kilter—you will not be able to deny it for very long. The flexibility will allow you to consider the possibility that your agitation is in *reaction* to something rather than in *response*. Then, it'll take strength to pull yourself back to be able to observe what's really going on for you.

As you know, agitation can take different forms. For example, when you get agitated you may suddenly become hot, your stomach may flutter, or it may feel like you got the wind knocked out of you—literally, an emotional explosion. That sort of agitation can be really obvious if you know to look for it. Agitation can also manifest as a nagging feeling, a disturbing or recurring thought, a short fuse, or conflicted emotions. Become aware of the patterns to your agitation so that when it occurs you can identify it for what it is. When you notice it, acknowledge it. Don't try to change it or make it go away or try to "talk yourself down." Simply acknowledging your agitation goes a long way in being able to deactivate it.

Also, be aware that agitation can be, and often is, sudden and unexpected. For instance, everything is going smoothly, and then something happens or someone says something and presto, you are bent out of shape. You just didn't expect it. Reactions like this often take us by surprise, but it helps to know that agitation happens and to be ready for it when it does.

Here are two examples of persistent, anticipated agitation:

◆ Virtually every time Linda's aunt Julie visits from out of state, the two women argue about one thing or another. Linda feels a certain level of agitation before the visit even begins, and she is on edge in all of their interactions. Unfortunately, the dis-ease between them is anticipated. It's never a surprise, but that doesn't make the confrontation any easier.

◆ When Louis gets behind the wheel, he is on high alert and is keenly aware of everything that is taking place on the road around him. He anticipates that the other drivers will "do something stupid or dangerous." When he does get cut off or someone fails to use his or her blinker or does something equally unlawful, Louis has an angry reaction and shouts at the other driver, even though the windows are closed and the other driver is a good distance away.

In these two cases, the agitation isn't unexpected. In this step of
GRACE, Linda and Louis simply need to be aware that an issue has
been activated and they are in reaction, which has resulted in agitation. In many ways, this sort of "expected" agitation is a setup, a self-
fulfilling prophecy. Dealing with their agitation *before* the encounters
would go a long way in creating a different, more harmonious outcome the next time they are in the situation.

Now consider this situation in which the agitation is unexpected:
Sarah is busy preparing a report when she learns that one of the vice
presidents is resigning from the company. Sarah believes she is qualified for the position, but then thinks that because she is a woman the
position will be scooped up by one of her male colleagues. A feeling of
foreboding overtakes her, and she can no longer see the report clearly.

Sarah is in reaction to the news and has become agitated. She's
already created a story. Her work here is to be aware that she has
become agitated. Because it was unexpected, she is less aware that she
is in reaction mode, so she needs to listen to her body's cues. For
instance, when she becomes agitated, Sarah's vision becomes blurry.
This is a key indication to her that something's presently out of whack.
"I can't even see clearly," she notices. "Something's going on here. I'm
agitated!"

STEP TWO: RECOGNIZE THE PATTERNS

In Chapter 3 we looked closely at how our patterns develop and how
they keep us operating within the same parameters despite our wanting to move beyond them toward more fulfilling life experiences and
relationships. Remember, there are different types of patterns to be
aware of: situational patterns, patterns in your agitation, and patterns
in your stories, all three of which we'll discuss in more detail on the
following pages.

So once you get agitated with awareness, the second step in
GRACE, the "R," is to *recognize the patterns*. This involves really exam-

How Soon Do You Recognize When You're Upset?

To ultimately deactivate your issue, you first need to know that the issue has been activated. Although this may seem like common sense, there will be times, at least in the beginning, when you think you have justifiably *responded* to a situation when in fact you have *reacted*. And it will only be later that you realize your issue had been activated. So, start noticing how soon you become aware that you are operating from an issue-activated position. With the awareness-enhancing exercises and techniques you've been engaging in throughout this process, you should have a good idea that an erro-

neous core belief has been activated and an emotional explosion has taken place. If you are in doubt, your body will help cue you in. Remember how your body feels when you get upset and be aware of what it is telling you while you are in the thick of things. Try to catch your agitation earlier and earlier each time.

ining yourself and your role in the situation at hand and recognizing how it fits into the patterns you've identified. Sometimes it will take a little investigative work to recognize your more subtle patterns.

What types of situations tend to activate your issue? In Louis's case, he gets activated when he goes out driving. That's his pattern: "I get agitated whenever I get behind the wheel." In Sarah's case, her pattern isn't as clear, but when she examines it, she recognizes that her pattern is to get agitated if she believes she is in competition with a man for something.

Is there a pattern to your agitation? For example, is it your pattern to get angry and belligerent, sad and weepy, passive-aggressive, withdraw, or lash out? How does your body react when it's agitated? What's the pattern there? Do you get hot or tense? Do you become short of breath? Do you "see red"? Does your back ache, head hurt, or neck get stiff? Do you feel sick to your stomach? Flush in the face? Do your ears ring? Does your jaw clench? Do you have a nervous tic? Does your blood pressure go up? Do your bowels start churning?

What are the patterns to your stories? Are you a victim? For example, the pattern to Louis's story is, "These drivers don't care about anyone but themselves and are putting me in danger!" The pattern to Sarah's story is that she has convinced herself that the man will always be the victor. In both cases, Louis and Sarah have labeled themselves as victims. Feeling like a victim is a red flag for anyone doing the work in this program.

What are the patterns to your distractions? Do you reach for a cookie or a glass of wine, or do you sit in front of the television watching several hours of inane sitcoms or murder mysteries while eating popcorn or ice cream (and, if that doesn't work, maybe both)? Maybe you go for a walk, take an exercise class, meditate, or keep yourself busy with work. Maybe you use your anger and/or stories as a distraction. For example, maybe you are ruminating over some perceived insult so that you do not have to face your own insecurities about yourself or a current situation. Whatever the case may be, knowing how you distract and the patterns to your distractions is important. This way, if you find yourself engaging in a patterned distraction, you can be certain that there is something to look at more closely.

Depending on where you are in the Frustration Cycle, you will likely have a recurring dominant physical and emotional reaction, which will feel very familiar to you. When you feel yourself reacting—in other words, when you are feeling these familiar physical and emotional symptoms—take note of what triggered you to react.

STEP THREE: ACCEPT FULL RESPONSIBILITY

It is not until you become agitated and recognize your patterns that
you start to realize that you alone are responsible for the feelings you
have about the situation. This then gives you the opportunity to move
forward in the process. You have reached the third step in GRACE,
the "A," *accept full responsibility* for the agitation and your patterns.
This doesn't mean you are blaming yourself; it simply means you are
not blaming anything outside of yourself. In other words, you are not
taking a victim stance. (Again, we're not talking about being a victim
of physical abuse or violence, see page 93.) If you find yourself saying
things like "My mother made me feel bad," "My sister hurt my feelings," "My boss made me feel stupid in front of my colleagues," and
so on, you have taken the victim stance. As soon as you hear yourself
saying things like "he or she *made me feel* . . . ," that's a red flag that
you are making someone else responsible for your agitation. You
alone are responsible for how you feel. When you can accept full
responsibility for what goes on inside you, you are one step closer to
the EXIT.

This might be a tough step for you to take. Accepting responsibility

for something—especially something attached to uncomfortable feelings—might feel counterintuitive. For example, you just know if so-and-so didn't say what she said, you wouldn't have lost so much sleep. If your ex-boyfriend didn't break up with you, you wouldn't be so depressed right now, and you wouldn't be crying into a bowl of ice cream or a glass of merlot. If your sister had respected your schedule, you wouldn't be missing the celebration. If your coworker didn't think she knew better than you, you wouldn't have to work so hard on a project you do not support. These thoughts keep going through your head, and you can't let them go. However, once you fully embrace this step, you'll realize that there's only one thing responsible for keeping you ruminating at night: *your issue.*

This is a very powerful step. It's not always going to be easy; in fact, it's probably never going to be easy. That's a big reason why our culture is so focused on placing the blame elsewhere. If everyone was able to accept responsibility for their own agitation, they could deal with whatever situation they were facing in a clear, intelligent, intuitive, and loving way, no matter what the situation might be. Again, this is about accepting responsibility for the issue activation. In order to live our life gracefully, powerfully, and successfully, we have to take responsibility for the fact that when we're upset it does not matter what the situation is, even if the situation looks dismal. It may *be* truly dismal. For example, we don't have enough money to pay our bills, or someone dear to us is ill. Or maybe there has been a natural disaster, or a terrorist attack, or some equally serious situation. If we're frightened and paralyzed and do not take responsibility for our feelings—in this case *fear*—we will end up running away or acting out of fear, and in doing so, it's unlikely we'll find a solution to the problem or be able to take the necessary action to improve the situation. So, once we accept responsibility for our agitation, we realize that we have the power to take whatever steps are necessary for a resolution to the problem either in the short term or long term, depending on the circumstances.

When you learn to accept responsibility, you become empowered.

ACCEPTING RESPONSIBILITY
FOR "WHERE" WE ARE

The "A" in GRACE is all about *accepting responsibility* for the agitation we are feeling and not distracting from it. But it's also important to accept responsibility for our place in life. The decisions we've made and the actions we've taken have all led us up to this point. We are here because we placed ourselves here. While there are certainly variables and things outside our control, it's important to realize that many of the situations we find ourselves in are of our own making. Plenty of people have "risen above their circumstances" or "beat all odds" to achieve personal success. These people took responsibility for their lot in life and still seized every opportunity to grow and change. That's not to say we all need a major overhaul—not at all. On a smaller scale, it's simply being aware that we play a big role in the situations in which we find ourselves because we've arrived there in whatever manner we went about doing so.

For example, think about your job. It didn't just happen to you; you applied for it, interviewed for it, and got the job. If you are married, you found someone with whom you proposed to spend the rest of your life and then entered into a marriage contract with that person. Again, you played a big part in that. If you are on a miserable vacation where nothing's going right, you are responsible for having chosen that destination, that "getaway package." Even if you are deceived by advertising claims and promises, you are still responsible for how you react to that situation. So in the majority of cases, wherever you find yourself, your own feet have done the walking to get there.

When we are in the loop of the Frustration Cycle, we might keep finding ourselves in some variation of a disagreeable situation. That's the nature of cycles: they return us to a place we've been before. When we accept responsibility for our part in arriving back at that same situational place or we accept responsibility for where we presently are in life, we have the opportunity to free ourselves because now we know we are not powerless to make changes.

Empowerment is a positive quality, while being a victim is always deflating. Practice taking responsibility for an upset; notice if you relax or tense up. Think of an agitating situation that didn't work out so well for you. How would things have been different if you had taken responsibility for the agitation? Here's an example with two possible outcomes:

After a scheduling mishap, Carol's Skype session with her life coach was rescheduled for three o'clock the following day. Carol readily accepted that scheduling mistakes happen, and while she was a bit disappointed, she gladly rescheduled. However, when 3:00 PM came and went the next day because the coach had once again made an error, Carol became agitated. She was experiencing an issue activation. Her issue, *There's no one there for me,* had been activated.

In scenario one, Carol gets angry with her coach for "not being there for her." *How could he just* forget *me? Twice in a row?* She also blames herself for being such a pushover. She has taken the stance of a victim. When her coach tries to reschedule, she tells him to just forget it. She refuses to reschedule and stews in her anger, unable to get anything else done for quite some time until she finally manages to distract herself with her work.

In scenario two, Carol gets agitated, but rather than blaming the coach and herself, she pauses. *Hmmm. I'm agitated,* she tells herself. *I have an empty pit in my stomach and my head feels hot. I feel uncared for.* She recognizes that she's experienced these manifestations of agitation before. Her pattern of stories, *how could he forget me* and *I'm such a pushover* aren't very convincing, because she knows they are not based in reality. She accepts responsibility for the feelings and accepts her coach's apology as well as his offer to add a half an hour onto her session free of charge while still making it clear, in a kind manner, that she was disappointed and inconvenienced. *Yes, let's reschedule again,* she agrees. With a clear head, she goes back to work and is very productive.

Do you see how Carol was empowered in the second scenario?

The situation occurred, and while it wasn't what Carol had planned, nothing she could do would change what happened. In this case, she was even rewarded with an extra half hour. Instead of being a victim, she accepted responsibility for the feelings and moved on, all to her benefit. There is a shift that takes place inside when you stop feeling victimized. Your physical energy literally gets a lift.

STEP FOUR: CURIOSITY

The fourth step in GRACE, "C," stands for *curiosity*. This step actually takes the place of distraction. In the Frustration Cycle, you have the situation and then you have the activation, which you eventually distract yourself from. Here, instead, you don't distract. You become curious. This step is where the real work begins and the point at which you can create transformation. Be aware, however, that it is very easy at this step to spiral back into being caught up in your issue-activated story; it can reignite your issue. Pay particular attention to the feedback you get from your body—for example, your breathing, the level of relaxation in your body, and other symptoms of agitation.

When curiosity has successfully taken over, you are very close to deactivating the issue: not concealing it, not suppressing it, not numbing it, not rationalizing it, and not falling victim to it. You're ready to be completely honest with yourself. This is when you have the courage to examine this question: "Where is my agitation *really* coming from?" This type of curiosity is innocent in nature. In other words, you are not trying to control the feelings or change them; you are simply becoming curious about what they really are.

Curiosity is always about the unknown, which is right below what you think you know. For example, Cynthia thinks she knows that all the men she dates are diverse characters, but when she begins making a list of their similarities, she realizes that she is consistently dating men who have a certain pattern of behavior that she finds annoying. This leads her to two additional questions to get curious about: why does she keep attracting men with this specific behavior pattern and why does this type of behavior annoy her?

Another client, Benjamin, attends monthly staff meetings, during and after which he consistently feels uncomfortable. Even though he doesn't drink alcohol during the week, on the evenings following his staff meetings he has a few drinks with dinner. He had always told himself that this was his reward for "putting up" with the meetings. However, when he got curious about his agitation during and after the meeting (his stomach would churn when the manager talked about deliverables, and he'd become fidgety and a bit tongue-tied when asked a question), he realized that his drinks were not rewards but distractions from his underlying feelings. In both cases, Cynthia and Benjamin needed to get curious about the agitating emotions they were feeling.

Curiosity also acts as the pause button, which we discussed on page 20. It creates a space between you and the circumstances or the object. You "pause the movie," jumping out of the situation and your story to see things from a different perspective, which is a place of more awareness. It gives you the opportunity to take note of (that is, get curious about) how your body is reacting to the situation. It's an opportunity for you to get curious about the stories you are telling yourself and to make a distinction between the situation and the story with the skills you've acquired throughout this program.

Get curious about the types of stories you are telling yourself as well: are they based on fact, on misinformation or not enough information, on memory, maybe even fantasy, and so on? Also, now that you've recognized the patterns, ask yourself what, where, when, and why the patterns happen. For example, Kirstin needed to ask herself why her patterned response to discussing uncomfortable topics, such as finances, with her husband always resulted in her running away from, or disengaging from, the situation. When they discussed the budget, she would feel criticized, become defensive, and react with anger. Her husband also had a predictable patterned reaction to this and would begin shouting, frustrated that the budget talk had once again turned sour. Not wanting to be yelled at further, Kirstin would leave the house. They would both end up distracting and suppressing until the next time.

In her work with us, Kirstin learned to get curious about why she was so affected by criticism and why she felt like she needed to run away from uncomfortable situations. She learned to employ GRACE as soon as she began feeling criticized and was eventually able to avoid running away from the argument. Kirstin's husband also learned that yelling was his pattern of reacting to her behavior and got curious about his role in the breakdown of the budget talks.

When you are working through step 4 of GRACE—curiosity— take the opportunity to also get curious about *where* you are in the cycle: situation, agitation, story, distraction, or suppression? Wherever you are in the cycle, that's where you will place your curiosity. This is a very powerful step because it allows you to jump out of the system and out of the cycle, and gives you the opportunity to get an overview of what's really going on inside of you. The goal of curiosity is to gain insight as well as "outsight." With insight (inward awareness), you will gain important information about the source of your agitation, which always comes from within. Your "outsight" (the application of your insight on the situational level) will clarify the situation and help you to respond accordingly.

The ultimate goal of this fourth step—becoming curious—is to be able to identify which issue is activated. Is your issue *I am alone?* What does it feel like? Does it feel like an empty pit in your stomach? Is it *There's not enough time?* Does it feel like a crushing weight on your shoulders, like backbreaking pressure? Maybe your head hurts. Is it *I'm not safe?* Do you feel on edge, a jumble of nerves, ready to sprint or hide away? Are you criticizing yourself? Is it *I'm not acceptable?* Do you feel like you're disgusting or wish you could shrink up and disappear? Is it *I'm not good enough?* Do you feel inadequate or wish you could just throw in the towel and let someone "more capable" handle it? Is it *I am unfulfilled*? Do you feel bored or inclined to go thrill seeking? Does your body feel sluggish or sleepy? Is it *I am not heard*? Is there tension in your neck? Maybe you feel hot. Is it *I am unable to trust*? Do you feel like you need to erect a stronger barrier between you and whatever you've encountered?

CURIOSITY JOURNALING EXERCISE

It's best to exercise the curiosity in GRACE while you're in the moment of agitation, but doing so takes some sincere diligence. If you are in reaction mode, it will be difficult at first to focus on how and why you are reacting, but you will get there with continued practice. Part of this practice could be looking back at a situation, your reaction, your distraction, and so on, and getting curious about each point in the cycle. Here's a good exercise that will help prepare you for the next time you're upset:

Take out your journal and draw the Frustration Cycle. Where it says "situation," insert one of your situational patterns. For example, let's say you are unhappy with a recent weight gain and you look in the mirror after getting out of the shower. That's the situation, and it occurs every time you get out of the shower. Now, how does that make you feel? Insert that next to "issue activation." *I feel bad, inadequate,* and so on. Which of the erroneous beliefs does that feeling best represent? *I'm not good enough?* What are the stories you are telling yourself about your weight? *I eat too much, I don't exercise enough,* and so on? Record whatever stories you tell yourself concerning the particular situation and issue you are examining here. Next, think about how you distracted yourself. For example, *I covered up with a towel* or *I thought about the day's upcoming events.* Again, insert whatever it is that you did to distract yourself from the particular past situation. Using the shower analogy, eventually you forget that you don't like the way you look, until

All of these are just examples, of course, but if you have trouble identifying your issue, this is a starting point. Get curious about your issue and these and similar questions. Reread the section on identifying your issue (see Chapter 3). Learn as much as you can about the "virus in your operating system." The more often you do this, the more easily it will come to you. For practice, you can look back at

---

the next day when again you get out of the shower. Journal about how your particular issue becomes suppressed within the cycle.

Doing this curiosity journaling exercise will give you more insight into how your issue drives your patterns within the Frustration Cycle so that you can more easily recognize an issue the next time it gets activated.

Here's another exercise that you can do in your journal to bring you further awareness through applying curiosity. When you are feeling agitated, respond to the following prompts in your journal:

- The emotion I'm experiencing is:

- Did I withdraw or power up?

- The situation is (just the facts):

- This is what I'm telling myself (my story):

- I feel _____ because of: _____

- The part or area of my body that is reacting is:

- This is what I wish would happen:

With these answers, you will have successfully distanced yourself enough from the situation, your story, and your agitation. This will allow you to pinpoint any residual agitation and give you an opportunity to further refine your curiosity. Do you now have a clearer view of what's happening? If there is no residual agitation, your job is to just relax, take it easy, and wait to see what happens next.

things that have happened in the past and get curious about what was at work there. See the curiosity journaling exercise on pages 126–127.

We can't emphasize enough that it doesn't help to try to get *rid* of your issue. As you know, that doesn't work; it simply keeps you rotating through the frustration loop. Instead, you want to deactivate the issue. Does that mean you will permanently deactivate the issue? No. But it can be rendered dormant for a time. Something *will* come along that activates it again, but when it does it will also come with a wonderful opportunity for change and growth. It's okay if you can't fully grasp this right now. Just know that as you practice the program, you will come to intimately understand how this dynamic operates.

So, what is the real method for deactivating the issue? When your curiosity transforms into compassion and you embrace your issue and make friends with it, you are consciously accepting what you subconsciously perceive to be your deepest flaw. When you examine the issue closely enough through earnest curiosity, you will discover that the very flaw that agitates you also keeps you striving for growth and change. Your inner relationship with that sore spot will change, and a new and deeper relationship with yourself will be nourished. This is your gift to yourself. This is your enlightening moment.

Yes, that's correct: the erroneous core belief that once limited you becomes your gift when you "turn it around" or view it from a new perspective. For years, perhaps a lifetime, you've been running away from those feelings, hoping to run fast enough to leave them behind, without realizing that those very feelings are also your strengths. The erroneous core belief, when it's embraced—that is, when you change your relationship to it—is part and parcel of your personality. It is the sensitive part of you that is absolutely perfect in its imperfection. Start tuning in to your hidden gift now. See your issue as an opportunity for further insight into situations that may have confused you in the past. Watch your issue transform into a strength that allows you to respond appropriately to the situations that used to be your place of self-undoing.

DEACTIVATING THE ISSUE, DISCOVERING YOUR GIFT

*In order to receive the gift,
you must carefully unwrap the present.*
—JEFFREY ARMSTRONG

Discovering your gift is the experience that allows you to deactivate the virus—the erroneous core belief that overrides all logic and intuition and feeds you inaccurate information about yourself. When you arrive at this step, you have all the tools that are necessary to build yourself a more fulfilling life. All of your relationships will deepen. Then you can continue the process, not just of preventing yourself from getting upset, but of learning how to become adept at deactivating any issue. Ultimately, the more you practice this and the more established your gifting ability becomes, the easier the entire process becomes.

Gifting could be a thought, a behavior, or an activity that gets to the core of the issue and turns it off rather than suppressing it. For example, maybe when you meditate, a wave of peaceful bliss comes across you and you feel very loving and kind toward yourself. That would be a gift. Perhaps the next time you are upset with yourself, you will cut yourself some slack and be gentle with yourself. You will realize, *Wow, I'm being really harsh with myself; let me back down,* and you immediately feel lighter. That's your gift. Maybe you have been butting heads with someone only to discover through gifting that there is no need to do so.

Gifts are very subtle, but when you find them, everything inside you goes, *Ahhhhhhhh.* Gifts give you clarity. When a gift arrives, you find that you are more accepting of things, perhaps something you were dead-set against. When a gift arrives, it comes with wisdom. You can understand the problem from a new perspective. When a gift arrives, your heart opens. You feel empathy, compassion, and love for everything around you. When a gift arrives, you know how to set boundaries without trying to control things. You are able to take care of yourself without being selfish. You will understand all this in a flash when a gift comes from deep inside you. You understand completely how to successfully navigate through a stressful situation. That's how important, and powerful, a gift is.

Your body will always lead you to a gift, but only if it is in a state of balance, and if it is flexible and strong. Deep breathing creates enough oxygen in the body that it triggers the centers in the brain and creates the chemicals in the body that allow you to be more available. You'll feel more. Your senses will work better. Your mind will be clearer. You will be a more empathetic being. You won't just try to figure things out with your mind. You can trust that the feelings will guide you. Remember, you can only arrive at this place by not trying to push away what's uncomfortable. Instead, you get curious about it and embrace it. The erroneous core belief is miraculously transformed. This is the gift of enlightening moments.

STEP FIVE: ENLIGHTENING MOMENT

When your curiosity results in *Aha!* rather than in more confusion, you will have discovered your hidden gift. You'll know this has happened because you will find yourself suddenly free of your agitation. The issue has been successfully deactivated for now. Something clicked, and you've regained your clarity. This step happens automatically when you have successfully performed the four steps before it. An *enlightening moment,* the "E" in GRACE, comes with the realization that the solution was there all along (in Chapter 6, we will discuss enlightening moments in-depth). You are suddenly more intuitive and receptive. The moment and circumstances are now more inviting, and you now have access to your innate wisdom and knowledge. You are receptive to hearing what you previously rejected. You are more available for invitations from the Universe.

There are no one-size-fits-all gifts in this process. Your gift—that which successfully deactivates your issue—is unique to you and what's going on inside you at that time. There's no magic bullet that is going to work each and every time you get activated, and you can't trade gifts with your friends. The gift is yours and yours alone. It is a deeper insight into the issue; it is an objective truth that suddenly makes everything crystal clear, and you will feel more connected to everything around you.

When you have reached this step, there is a shift or change in your perspective, and your relationship to whatever you had been focusing on is suddenly transformed. Your awareness has reached a pinnacle, and you are fully present to the moment.

When you experience an enlightening moment, every cell in your body comes alive with each of the five senses functioning to their fullest capacity. This results in a heightened physical sense of yourself and your surroundings. Clients have reported that, in a flash, they have gone from a state of confusion over how to handle a difficult interaction with someone at work to a sudden diffusion of the situation accompanied by the ability to effortlessly move the process forward. Many couples who have practiced GRACE with each other share that their reactions do not necessarily disappear, but that they are capable of responding to each other with more compassion and understanding of the other person's dilemma. The resulting empathy creates a stronger bond and encourages further communication.

However, it's important to know that not all enlightening moments have storybook endings. In many situations, learning how to experience sadness, disappointment, anger, and other emotions is the only possible endpoint. An enlightening moment is not another distraction to be used as a way to reach a resolution without dealing with the situation. Instead, it provides you with more clarity with which to approach and resolve the situation, which may include experiencing the full extent of whatever is taking place within you and around you.

There are many approaches to temporarily deactivating the issue; however, it is important to note that all deactivations are just that— momentary pauses that allow you to learn how to prepare for the next time agitation happens. The situations that act as catalysts do not necessarily disappear just because you have learned how to relax during them. On the contrary, success in life is conditional on knowing how to take on the challenges and remain balanced, flexible, and strong, no matter how intense circumstances may become.

Enlightening moments open a channel of wisdom that is immediately tested. There are no guarantees in this process that your desires will be met or your goals achieved. Just because you are no longer agitated (that is, your issue has been deactivated) does not mean that everything will be the way you would like it to be. It is possible to experience disappointment and other similar emotions without being in the issue-activated state. In fact, when you are fully available to experience all the uncomfortable emotions, you will learn, grow, and feel more secure in your whole life. However, rewarding conclusions are always delightful when we've worked so hard to achieve them.

JOURNEY WITH GRACE: A RECAP

Let's go through GRACE again. No matter where you are in the Frustration Cycle, you can take the following steps to reach an exit. "G" stands for *get activated*. That's step one. You don't need to find your gift if you're not activated. These are the moments in your life when you are loving and compassionate with yourself, others, and the world around you. You are feeling fulfilled and satisfied from within. Unfortunately, some people never feel this way. But for most of us, life is a continuum, a kind of like a roller coaster. We're feeling good; there are no issue activations. Then boom! Something happens and we are suffering and soon distracting ourselves. So getting activated with awareness is the process that begins your journey of dealing with your upsets, dissatisfaction, loneliness, distrust, inability to be successful, and so on. When you journey with GRACE, you're ready to find the solution to the issue activation. And the solution is a graceful movement toward finding your gift.

Step two, "R," is to *recognize the patterns* at play in the issue activation. You recognize that you are upset, but you also acknowledge that you've felt this way before under similar circumstances. You recognize that you've taken these actions before. Some cycle is at play here. This is not a new situation, not a new feeling, not a new story. It's important that upon recognizing the patterns, you take the next step to the "A" in GRACE: *accepting responsibility* for the agitation and the patterns. Too many people want to remain at "R." They recognize that they're upset and that this is a recurring theme, but they are so caught up in the Frustration Cycle that they still try to blame the situation, which may include blaming themselves or others. So in order to accept responsibility, it's essential to recognize that we have an erroneous core belief that is now corrupting our ability to clearly, accurately, and successfully respond to the situation.

Accepting responsibility is key. We hope that with all the practices, recommendations, and tools that we've shared with you up to this

point, you'll be willing to accept responsibility for the issues in
your life. If you are upset, accept responsibility for being upset. Okay,
someone has done an unkind thing, and you have had a reaction to it.
We're not saying that you should accept responsibility for their behavior, but rather, you're accepting responsibility for your reaction to their
behavior. You are acknowledging that their behavior has activated
your issue and has brought it to the sur-
face, but that person is not responsible
for creating your erroneous core belief.
Once you accept responsibility for being
upset because something inside of you
is being triggered, you will not project
blame onto the other person or the situation itself and thereby obsure
and exacerbate the agitation. Instead, you realize that you will never
find your gift that way. The best you'll be able to do is to distract and
suppress, knowing your agitation will pop up to the surface again
when you least expect it, like a beach ball you've been trying to hold
underwater.

> *Turning up the light of
> awareness helps illuminate
> the previously hidden
> cause of your agitation.*

So, after accepting responsibility for being upset, the next step is
the defining moment. The next step is going to bring you to a place
where your gift appears. This step is the big "C": *curiosity*. You want to
get curious about your agitation, stories, and patterns—anything that's
going on deep within. What is your emotional reaction when your
issue activation is present? What is the physical experience? What is
the emotional experience? Are you using absolute words, such as
always and *never*? When we use absolute terms, it's a pretty clear indication that our perception is corrupt. That is a clue regarding what
you want to get curious about. The more curiosity you bring into this
step, the further removed you are from being controlled by the erroneous core belief, giving you the clarity that distance affords. This is
not distracting from it or suppressing it. This is distancing from it so
that you can view it more objectively. This is an essential distinction. If

you distract, you are only going to suppress the issue and try to push it down and out of sight until it finally pops up again. So this time, when it comes up, you get curious about it. Curiosity comes from the aware part of you. Curiosity is your "knower self," that purest state of consciousness that doesn't judge, evaluate, or analyze; it just sees clearly what's really going on. You're now allowing yourself to stay fully present to your issue, and by not running away from it, you're changing your relationship to it.

Be aware that when you become curious like this, you have achieved a remarkable feat. Most people in the world are trying to distract themselves and avoid their uncomfortable feelings, but now you are facing yours head-on. You are standing up to the "bully" inside you. We simply can't buy enough, consume enough, eat enough, medicate enough, or blame others enough to deactivate our issue. As a matter of fact, engaging in these distractions and others like them only deepens that groove. So instead of doing all of that, you're not going to distract anymore. You're going to accept responsibility for and be curious about the truth of why you are upset. While you are doing this, you're still going to be in some state of reaction. But instead of suppressing it, you are now embracing it. This takes practice. But it is a powerful step.

Once that curiosity reaches a certain threshold, you're going to experience a release. You will feel the issue deactivate and begin to dissolve. You just changed your relationship to it, and you did it on purpose. You embraced it. This will lead to your hidden gift, a period in your experience where everything is perfect, and it is perfect because you're not trying to manipulate and control it from an agitated state. You now have more confidence. You trust yourself. You begin to trust the world around you. You trust your ability to pay attention to the details and know what's best. You have had an *enlightening moment,* the "E" in GRACE. You have successfully taken this part of your journey with GRACE.

Linda and Keith's Experience

FINDING THE GIFT

 Although Linda and Keith had done a lot of work on their relationship and marriage, they had different ways of looking at things; they were also both strong-minded. This was a good recipe for lively and long-lasting arguments that got them nowhere. As soon as they began butting heads, their issues would get activated and neither would be willing to do the work in the heat of the moment. To help them out, they were given a tool that I believed would immediately deactivate the issue for one or both of them: the common hug. Their task was to hug each other the moment they started butting heads.

Linda says, "It took a long time for me to actually use this tool. In the moment I wanted to rip his head off. Often when we get into an argument, it's because the person closest to us is out of balance and they take it out on us. Then we get sucked into it and get thrown off balance too. We often take it personally and then the argument escalates. Since I have a pretty feisty personality, I usually go into defense mode and have to win! Giving a hug to someone who has seemingly just attacked me was not something I learned growing up."

Linda knew that Keith was not responsible for her agitation, so she worked on GRACE whenever she got activated, but it still took her six months to finally be able to carry out the assignment. She'd just finished the tedious job of cleaning shrimp for the evening's dinner and put them in the strainer in the sink. Just then, Keith stormed into the room in a serious off-balance moment (having just lost a client), and he flung the shrimp out of the strainer. Normally, Linda would have gotten sucked in, thrown off balance, and shouted at him. However, she quickly deactivated her own issue. She got agitated with awareness, recognized that her standard pattern wouldn't bring about the harmony she desired, accepted responsibility for the agitation (his behavior wasn't personal, it was just her reaction to the behavior), quickly moved through the curiosity of what issue had become activated (*there's something wrong with me*), and became curious about how out of balance he was. Thus, she arrived at the enlightening moment where she was able to take Keith in her arms. Upon feeling her sincere love through this gesture, his anger about losing a client immediately melted away, and they stood in a loving embrace for several moments.

"It was the most freeing moment of our relationship, and I finally understood what you had been training me to experience," Linda later told me. "We used to hold on to our anger so tightly, allowing arguments to last for days. But now when we butt heads, our arguments dissipate quickly. And instead of holding on to anger, we hold on to each other." This is the gift of GRACE.

Note in this case, after deactivating her own issue, Linda became curious about Keith's issue activation, which permitted her natural empathy to shine through. The Experience for the Road (on page 138) will help you learn how to turn your curiosity into compassion for those around you once your own issue has been deactivated through GRACE.

❧ Mock-Agitation Exercise ❧

Think for a moment about the physical manifestations of agitation: shortness of breath, tightness in the chest, mental fogginess, muscle tension, increased body temperature, and so on. Some of these physical symptoms are very similar to how you might feel after aerobic exercise. Usually after exercise, you have some time to cool down and catch your breath, but when these symptoms come on suddenly as manifestations of your agitation—for example, in a meeting—you don't have the same cool-down period available to you. You need to learn to bring your body back into balance right away, and this is accomplished through taking control of your breath.

To practice regaining your composure on the spot, cause yourself some "mock agitation" with the following two exercises:

1. Elevate your heart rate for at least ten minutes through your preferred method of aerobic exercise. Then stop and see how many deep, three-part breaths it takes to return your breathing to normal. (Be sure you've become adept at the Breathing for Awareness Exercise in Chapter 1; see page 30.) The ultimate goal is to slow your breathing to a non-agitated state within three repetitions.

2. Gently spin around twelve times until your equilibrium is a bit off-kilter. (Be sure to have plenty of room so you don't bump into anything.) Stop, unlock your knees, and focus your attention on an object that is at eye level. Again, do the three-part breath. As before, the ultimate goal is to slow your breathing to a non-agitated state in three repetitions.

In both cases, keep a record in your journal of the count of your inhalation and exhalation. Each time you engage in these exercises, try to improve your count. Also, try to improve the number of breaths it takes to return your breathing to normal. These exercises will strengthen your body through longer exhalations, increase your balance by helping you regain your equilibrium more quickly, and help to keep your body from tensing up, thereby keeping you flexible. Then, the next time you are agitated, use this practice to your advantage to regain your composure on the spot so that you are in a better position to practice GRACE on the spot and respond to the situation as necessary.

❧ Experience for the Road ❧

Now that you are in the process of practicing GRACE when you become agitated and have had success deactivating your issue at least in some situations, you can start turning your attention outward and begin to notice and get curious about other people's agitation. Take an educated guess about what their issue activation might be. Do this only if you are not activated yourself. Begin watching your friends, family, and coworkers in various situations and take note when tempers flare, tears come, angry words pass their lips, and so on. Become curious about what's going on beneath the surface. Which virus do you think has temporarily taken control of their operating system?

This practice is not intended to give you the upper hand in an argument, to label the other person in some negative way, or to encourage you to share your observations with them. Rather, getting curious about their issue activation gives you the opportunity to practice compassion and to offer them a silent gift by responding in a comforting way. Also, it gives you an opportunity to check your own *reaction* to their words or behavior and to transform that reaction into a GRACE-ful response.

Be sure to record these experiences in your journal. You will observe that your insight into these matters grows deeper the more often you practice. Your awareness of when you and others are operating from a less than optimal place will even help you reverse course if necessary to allow you to flow more easily with the challenges and opportunities that unexpectedly present themselves to you.

You've come a long way since the beginning of this journey, and we are so pleased to have had the opportunity to share GRACE with you. The more often you journey with GRACE, the more often you will experience the delight of knowing that in the long run everything is right with the universe and that you can flow through life much more easily and gracefully. This doesn't mean you will never become agitated. But soon you will look at your feelings of agitation as a portal toward a deeper understanding of yourself and the world around you. In the next chapter, we'll look at how pleasant life can be when experienced through a series of enlightening moments.

CHAPTER 6

Enlightening Moments
Being Available to Everything

There is in all visible things a hidden wholeness.
—THOMAS MERTON

As you've learned throughout this book, when we experience a situation, one of two things can happen: we can *respond* or we can *react*. It doesn't matter if the situation is positive, negative, or neutral. When we respond, we simply experience the situation for what it is and have certain feelings as part of a natural, organic response. We're in balance. We're flexible. And we have strength to respond in whatever manner is necessary. We're handling the situation very well. We're focused. Our mind is strong. We hold our ground and set boundaries as necessary. So, no matter from which direction the wave comes, we will be able to ride it well, moving our weight on the board as needed to ride the wave wherever it may take us. Our awareness is expanded and we are open for whatever may come.

The other possibility is that we *react* to a situation by operating from an explosion inside of us, which, as you know, is our issue-activated spot, or I-spot. This explosion clouds our mind, and our awareness becomes hazy. As you now understand, it's desirable to *respond* to situations, not *react* to them, which you will begin doing almost automatically once you become more adept at journeying with

GRACE. It's from this place of response that you are more open to experiencing enlightening moments (without having to work through all of the steps). We all know they exist, and we all want to experience them. In fact, every human action is routed in an attempt to experience them, but now you know how to prepare yourself for them. In this chapter, let's take a closer look at what they are all about so we can arrive at a deeper understanding of how to invite graceful moments into our life more often.

An Experience Beyond Words

We could write until there are no more words in the dictionary, but no amount of explanation can adequately describe how it *feels* to experience an enlightening moment. This is an experience beyond words, but we've been doing our best to help you prepare for those precious moments when they happen. Rest assured, when you experience one, you will be keenly aware of it. We've all experienced an enlightening moment on some level from time to time throughout our lives, so when you do experience that *Aha!* moment, however brief it may be, you will recognize it and know it as intimately as you would an old friend.

HOW DO ENLIGHTENING MOMENTS HAPPEN?

As you've probably deduced, you cannot "do" an enlightening moment. An enlightening moment does you. It's impossible to make it or will it to happen. Even if you follow all the early steps in GRACE, there's no guarantee that you are going to have that *Aha!* moment we've been discussing. When attempting to deactivate your issue, it is only through finding your gift that you will experience the "E" in GRACE. It may be momentary and it may be delayed, but once you find that gift and deactivate your issue, you will experience that moment of clarity, that long, comforting sigh of release.

> *An enlightening moment doesn't mean that you have everything you want or need and that everything is the way you think it should be. You will probably never have everything you want or need, and things will probably never be exactly how you want them to be. An enlightening moment goes beyond wants, needs, and thoughts, and trying to control a situation to fit your expectations. Here, everything is exactly as it is without judgment. You have achieved a sense of clarity, a deeper understanding of the world through direct, unencumbered experience.*

However, it isn't only through the five steps of GRACE that enlightening moments happen. As we've mentioned, the steps of GRACE are only necessary when you find yourself stuck and unable to work your way out of an agitating situation. In fact, Radha and I live much of our life traveling from moment to moment where everything is exactly as it should be, including when things do not go according to our plan. You can live that way too, but like we said, you can't force it to happen. What you can do, however, is prepare yourself to be receptive to those moments. And that comes with following the program in this book, practicing the exercises, participating in the Experiences for the Road, journaling often, and generally keeping yourself aware of what's going on inside and around you.

It is like carefully cultivating a seed—you can pretty much be assured that someday it will grow into the plant it's intended to be. When you've prepared the soil and have provided all of the necessary conditions it needs, the seed will sprout. With the right care, that seed will grow into a healthy plant. It will need continued care, of course, to keep it flourishing. Likewise, the seed you have planted within yourself will respond to the environment in which it's placed. When your environment is free of explosions and distractions, you have the capacity for more awareness, which leads to seeing the world from a more objective perspective. You are fully present—body and mind—and it is always a touching and *meaning-full* experience. Here, you will be able to experience its beauty and imperfections with compassion, understanding, joy, and love. When we begin to relax around all of those things that once caused us so much grief, pain, and suffering, we make ourselves more available for the lessons we need to learn. This comes with transforming our relationship with our issue, with the parts of us that are not perfect. So again, we don't make enlightening moments happen; they just do . . . but only if we are good gardeners and have prepared ourselves to be open for them to bloom.

RECOGNIZING AN ENLIGHTENING MOMENT

Enlightening moments are small, constant things that occur in a big way. Angels will not always trumpet their arrival. There will likely be no ringing bells or flashing lights. You may experience them suddenly or spontaneously or it may take days (or longer) of exercising curiosity for your gift to arrive. Be ready for it and be careful of the tendency to later attach it to something outside of yourself. Remember, it came from somewhere deep within you. You know the experience firsthand; it's that feeling of incredible awe. Perhaps you've felt this way, for instance, at the birth of a baby, overlooking a vast mountain range, hearing the roar of thunder as the whole house shakes with its power, witnessing a sunset or a sunrise, watching ominous storm clouds roll in, seeing an eagle flying overhead, being present when someone dear to you passes, suddenly realizing that you feel love for a companion, finding the solution to a puzzle, noticing "coincidences" and the connection between things . . . we could go on and on, for GRACE is all around and everywhere within us.

As you know, these moments are usually fleeting; the experience is so big and so incredible and perfect that you want to hold on to it

THE WAITING ROOM

If you diligently practice exiting the Frustration Cycle whenever you become agitated, you'll eventually arrive in the waiting room—that place where you simply sit and wait for your appointment with the specialist. You can't barge into the doctor's office and demand to be seen that moment. No, instead, you wait patiently for your name to be called. You've done everything to get yourself to your appointment. You've completed filling out the forms and reflected on the questions, and now the next step is out of your control. And that's okay. It is as it should be. For some appointments you wait longer than others, but that's okay too. Your only task is to just wait; that clarifying moment when the door opens and your name is called *will* come. And everything will light up inside you as you stand to greet the moment.

and re-create it. However, in trying to re-create these moments, what you'll discover is that each is so unique that they cannot be duplicated. They sit in your memory reminding you of the possibilities ahead. So again, take care not to attach the moment to a limited external event. Simply be aware of the potential of each new moment within you.

Here's an example: You are on vacation, and you have no worries clouding your mind, no pressing obligations. You sit on the balcony overlooking the ocean to watch the sunset. Your mind is clear. The colors are magnificent and you are filled with incredible light. You are fully available to the moment, everything inside you is silent and perfect, and the world is exactly as it should be. Then, the sun dips below the water. The moment lingers, then passes. The next night, you expect to experience the same feeling when you watch the sunset. But you are thinking about the day's events and whether or not you made reservations for dinner and so on. What you don't realize is that it wasn't the sunset that "caused" your enlightening moment. It was the clarity you experienced when you were watching the sunset because you were fully present to the moment, not somewhere lost in your thoughts of yesterday or tomorrow. That is the *power of now* that Eckhart Tolle refers to in his book by the same name. Being present to the moment opens up a world of perfect possibilities.

> Enlightening moments are always perfect—even when they don't meet our expectations.

Our culture has been conditioned into thinking that fulfillment can be found outside ourselves by purchasing big-ticket items, taking exotic vacations, or through having other external pleasurable experiences. We have been trained to attach that feeling of contentment to material things or experiences. But we can't emphasize enough that it is not necessary to be on vacation or be doing anything to find fulfillment. We can be fully present to every moment—good, bad, or indifferent—no matter where we are, and find within those moments the clarity that is present without distractions. When an enlightening moment happens, as long as you don't try to attach it to the circumstances surrounding it, it doesn't matter what's going on outside of you; it occurs inside, and you will know it from within through your awareness.

BEING FULLY AVAILABLE TO FEEL THE EMOTION OF AN EXPERIENCE

Many people are under the mistaken impression that if we don't experience intense emotional explosions that run the gamut from extreme pleasure to unbearable pain that we aren't truly experiencing life. But this, of course, is a fallacy. An emotion doesn't have to be an explosion for it to be felt very deeply in its purest form. In fact, not only are we rational human beings, but we are also emotional creatures, empathic beings, who navigate life by *feeling* our way. When our minds are clear and free of issue activations, our intuition (our innate knowingness) helps us move through life easily, naturally, and safely. We put out our "tentacles" and feel for the next right thing to do, and we do it without overanalyzing it or creating stories around it. The more we are issue-activated or the bigger our issue activation is, the less intuition we have available, and so we end up wearing a blindfold and struggling to get through the chain of events that occur throughout an ordinary (or less than ordinary) day. From this issue-activated state, we search for only pleasurable experiences, avoiding emotions such as fear, anger, or sadness, distracting ourselves from them as if they were enemies from which we need to escape. All of our emotions are useful and necessary, however, and when experienced from a nonissue-activated state, emotions such as anger, fear, and sadness are actually there to help us take the necessary action to positively contribute to a situation, to protect us from harm, to use our discrimination wisely, and so on.

Throughout this process, you've been learning to "make friends" with emotions you find uncomfortable, those from which you distract yourself. You know from reading this book that this is the only way out of the Frustration Cycle. Think now about the distractions that you have turned to in the past to bury your uncomfortable feelings. How would your life change without these distractions? How would *you* change? Reevaluate your distractions and differentiate between what is an activity you simply enjoy and one that you use to distract yourself. Remember, it's the intention with which you engage in an activity that determines whether or not you are using it as a distraction. In other words, distractions are not necessarily what you do but the state of consciousness in which you do them. The less you engage in distractions and the more awareness you bring to the situation and to your inner being, the more your negative patterns will begin to unravel, freeing you to expand your consciousness and thereby experience life more deeply in whatever manner it reveals itself. You will flow with the river that runs through your life, rather than struggle to stay afloat. Better to go with the current than try to swim against it.

STILL WELCOMING THE AGITATION . . .

In the quote at the beginning of Chapter 5, we said that we look forward to the next time we get agitated. This may sound contrary to what one might expect from people who normally go with the flow of higher awareness, but we know we are not superhuman. Issues can only be deactivated, not destroyed. If we were to destroy them, we would be destroying an important—even essential—part of ourselves. We'd be looking a gift horse in the mouth, so to speak. While issue activations happen infrequently for us, we know that they will happen, and when they do, we have an opportunity to further expand our awareness of ourselves and our understanding of life and its relationships. So, yes, we welcome the opportunity to practice GRACE whenever it presents itself. We may not welcome issue activations with open arms, shouting, "Hurray! I'm issue-activated again!" but we recognize the importance of the practice. And we know that we will grow as a result. This is like an athlete who practices his or her sport in extreme conditions. All the concentrated and dedicated effort an athlete puts into the preparation of the big game pays off the most when he or she performs under adverse conditions. In the same way, we prepare ourselves through practice for living life as consciously as possible as human *beings,* not just human *doings.*

ENLIGHTENING MOMENTS BEYOND THE GIFT

When we operate from a place of awareness, we are prepared and ready for the endless possibilities that will present themselves. We will not be limited by concepts. We can exceed what we once thought were our limitations. We are fully available emotionally to whatever feelings are present, and we can respond to whatever is happening appropriately and constructively. It is possible to travel from one enlightening moment to the next in a string of events that flow like a fresh stream down the side of a lush green mountain on a bright summer's day. In this way, our intuition, our intellect, and our sensitivity to the environment are unencumbered and function at their optimal levels for the greater good. Some of the greatest insights, solutions to problems, or inspiration arrive at such times. Each step we take is revealed to us as we take it. Things that we might have thought were merely coincidences suddenly seem to be put in place in accordance with a grand plan or some Divine Guidance, leading us to exactly where we need to be. In this way, enlightening moments can become an unending stream of wonder-filled experiences. Our days flow naturally and our attachment to whether or not we accomplished such and such a thing or did such and such a thing simply drop away. The day simply unfolds as it is meant to unfold. This doesn't mean that we don't make plans or set goals. Instead, those plans and goals are accomplished without struggle and with loads of grace. This is our natural state of consciousness.

❧ The Receptivity Exercise ❧

This exercise is best practiced during the day in a brightly lit, colorful room. When you have some time to yourself and you have no pressing obligations, find a comfortable seat and practice the Breathing for Awareness Exercise on page 30. Breathe until you feel very relaxed, and then close your eyes for a few moments. When you open your eyes, do not concentrate on anything. Keep your eyes softly focused just ahead of you. Allow the colors in the room to envelop you. Without labeling things, notice the shapes in the room and the different textures as well as the different colors. Simply be receptive and open to the information that is coming in from your perceptions. The object of this exercise is to become aware of the difference between forming an opinion about an object and merely allowing your senses to absorb information about it. This experience of being present in the now is what we call *direct perception.* When this occurs, memory and analysis take a second-row seat to being fully present in the moment-to-moment experience of reality.

❧ Experience for the Road ❧

As you go throughout your day, try jump-starting your enlightening moments. As long as you are not having a major issue activation, you can run through GRACE pretty quickly, turning even the slightest upsets into stepping-stones. Sometimes, it can be as simple as changing your story. For example, if you are running late to an appointment and are stopped at a red light, think about how stopping at that light has just changed the course of your day. Perhaps it's kept you from a minor fender bender in the parking lot when you arrive at your destination. Also, toy with the notion that being late to an appointment is not the end of the world, and it might in fact be the pause you need to remind you that certain things are beyond your control, or maybe it is a much-needed lesson in time management. That's just one example. Many such examples present themselves to us frequently over the regular course of the day. These things may seem to interfere with the natural flow of things, but it is actually our distorted perceptions that interfere with this flow.

Notice your emotional responses or reactions to things. If you are simply responding emotionally in a clearheaded manner, there's no need to do anything. But if you are having a reaction to something that's not going the way you expected, turn it around so that you are looking at it from a new, positive perspective. For instance, if someone cancels plans with you at the last minute, tell yourself that you are now free to do something else, like read that book you've been saving (or better yet, write that book you know is trying to come out). Notice if there is a shift in awareness when you put a positive spin on things. Notice if you expand or contract. If you expand, great. If you contract, look a little deeper. Keep a record of your observations in your journal.

Everything we do as human beings is an effort to achieve the state of serenity as it's been described in this chapter, a place where we feel at peace with the world and ourselves, even if we aren't consciously aware that is what we're doing. If we don't know how to achieve that state, if we have no guidance, we can easily get stuck in the endless loop of dissatisfaction, as we've described throughout this book. Fortunately, our practice and experience has made it possible for us to guide you along this journey toward deeper awareness. You now know that the awareness is within you, and it has been there all along. You also know that enlightening moments are available and how to prepare yourself to receive their endless invitations and gifts.

Conclusion

Why would anyone want to be more aware?
—COUSIN JOEY

In the beginning of this book, I described an experience my cousin Joey and I had shared one afternoon after he and my dad had gone on a fishing trip. Joey asked me what I do exactly, and I carefully responded that I help people become more aware. And, well, you know what Joey wanted to know next: *Why would anyone want to be more aware?*

As soon as Joey's question left his lips, I was acutely aware that this is the dilemma that every human being faces. People have spent so much time in their life distracting themselves from their uncomfortable emotions that they believe becoming more in tune with what they are feeling will create even more pain, so they continue to distract themselves as a way of life. This further decreases their awareness, and they become accustomed to limping toward the pot of gold at the end of the rainbow or worse. Because they lack awareness, they look to others to tell them what's right or wrong. They are disconnected from their own intuitive wisdom and have lost trust in themselves and the natural order of the universe.

I looked at Joey, and said, "Well, Joey, that's a good question." Then I briefly explained to him that it's important to be aware of things, such as if someone like our child or wife needs us, or if we have a health issue that needs attention, or if there's an accident up ahead and we need to slow down to avoid the pileup, and so on.

Joey shook his head in agreement, as I went on to say, "When we are aware of small problems, we can keep them from growing into larger problems. When there are no secrets or hidden agendas, our actions will not be hindered by what we don't know. We can respond to everything the way we are meant to rather than react from a place of not knowing. Awareness allows us to experience our lives more fully and more completely."

So Joey just looked at me, thought about it for a moment, and said, "I get it. Like with my business, if one of my clients is unhappy, I'm gonna wanna know about it . . . be *aware* of it."

"Exactly," I replied. "If you aren't aware of your customer's dissatisfaction, how can you make any changes or reparations?"

In that moment, the light bulb over his head suddenly got bright. "Ah," he said, as his whole body relaxed. In his own way, Joey had an enlightening moment, or so it seemed. His response to my explanation caused his whole body to relax as he came to understand why Radha and I place such importance on *being aware*.

Okay, it's true we weren't talking about the depth of awareness discussed in this book, but it was a good start for a caring, loving guy like my cousin Joey. Without being aware, we do not learn from our mistakes, we miss countless opportunities, we suffer needlessly, our underused mental faculties weaken as we age, and, worst of all, we are consigned to repeat the lower grade levels of life lessons over and over again.

Awareness is the engine that runs the universe. People who are unaware live in an agitated state without ever knowing the real cause of their dissatisfaction and unrest. Out of necessity, they are bound to distract themselves. Like a rebellious third grader, they would rather play video games than study for tomorrow's spelling test. We think of birth into this world as entering a university, one with grade levels specifically designed to the degree of awareness we bring to each course. If we increase our awareness, we do not need to repeat the lower grades that are replete with life's many struggles. If we have not yet learned how to remain aware in the face of fear, loneliness, anger, and other uncomfortable emotions, then with extraordinary precision, the University of Life gives us yet another opportunity to "get it." I keep the following quote on my desk:

In school you take the lesson first, and then get the test.
In life you take the test first and then get the lesson.
—AUTHOR UNKNOWN

It's been a delight to share our approach with you throughout these pages. I hope we have the opportunity someday to share more of our teachings with you. Good luck on your journey. Radha and I send our love and our best wishes for many enlightening moments ahead.

Enlightening Moments with GRACE

GEORGE'S ENLIGHTENING MOMENT WITH GRACE

Upon returning home from a long day of meetings, George was once again faced with an all-too-familiar dilemma. He'd been feeling pretty elated over the successful year-end reports that showed profits higher than expected. Then the phone call came. He had been putting off getting back to his friend who had requested yet another loan that would add to an already large sum still owed, which made George's chest tighten. George had worked through his issue in the past and did not want to fall back on his old patterns; he began to agonize over how he would deal with the situation.

Even though he had given his friend money previously without expecting it to be returned, he could not quiet his mental chatter. On the one hand, his story about how he was being used kept coming up, and, on the other hand, he couldn't shake his guilty feelings for not giving in immediately. He sat down in his home office feeling restless. He felt drained of the positive memories of the day and suddenly began wondering which girlfriend he should invite out for a celebratory evening on the town. He quickly recalled that dating was one of his ways of distracting himself from uncomfortable feelings. Already having gotten good at exiting the Frustration Cycle, George knew that he would need to practice GRACE and not distract himself from the issue. He felt angst at being in this same frustrating situation once again.

For George, the most difficult part of his situation was believing that his friendship could be saved if he just gave his friend the money—after all, helping others always made him feel good. But he knew that wasn't the answer. Instead of reacting or distracting, George listened to a relaxation CD, and then meditated and practiced his breathing techniques. Finally, he recognized the pattern: he just wanted the situation to be over with at any cost! Recognizing that made him realize just how big this activation really was. Since George had been getting really good at the lesser activations, he was pumped up to face this one. His pattern of throwing money at a problem would be an easy fix. The more difficult path would be for George to accept responsibility that his friend was unaware of how uncomfortable his request made him. "What's the matter with him? Couldn't he see that I was making a lame excuse about having to think about it? Anyone could see how uptight I was with the request!" George had said those very words on more than one occasion, but he never actually told his friend that the request for money made him feel uneasy.

George finally accepted full responsibility for the fact that he did not stay strong in the face of discomfort. He admitted that it felt horrible to not be honest with someone. He had the highest integrity of anyone around, and this one cut to the core.

Next, he had to get his curiosity awakened. This pushed him to the limit of awareness, as it does to many of my clients. He began exploring the different responses possible in order to maintain the friendship and set a boundary. It was during this process that he realized that caving in and loaning his friend the money was actually enabling his friend's issue to remain suppressed.

George's review of the Frustration Cycle allowed him to clearly see that helping his friend was his distraction. If he gave him the money, he could quickly, but only for the moment, suppress the feeling of loneliness and the debilitating agitation of feeling that something was wrong with him. This situation had clearly activated both of his major issues.

George's enlightening moment came after an intimate conversation with his friend at his friend's house. He spent an hour beforehand meditating on what was best for both of them. He wanted to employ the same strategy that had made him extremely successful in his professional life: he wanted a win-win solution.

After a few false starts, his chest relaxed, his breath grew deeper, and a wave of ease passed over him as he looked his friend in the eye and shared that there was something so much bigger at play than his friend's financial dilemma. By being honest about what was going on for him, George allowed his wisdom and compassion to shine forth, which permitted his friend to relax, listen, and reflect on the content of the conversation.

The enlightening moment was sudden and compelling. His friend's eyes moistened; George sat back in the chair, also feeling the emotional content present in the room. They both fell silent for a moment before a two-hour conversation began. George was able to give expert advice regarding the steps his friend could take to deal with the actual reason he was relying on George to bail him out once again. His friend shared how painful it was to beg for money and thanked George for his helpful advice.

As George left for home that evening, he was elated. Although still experiencing a fair degree of sadness for the financial challenges that lay ahead for his friend, George relished his state of physical relaxation, mental clarity, and the ease with which he was feeling such strong emotions. It turned out that the friend was touched by George's support and sought out a business coach who, for the next year, helped him learn how to support his family and business.

What began as another painful encounter with his issue resulted in a closer friendship with mutually agreed-upon financial boundaries. Now, every time George mentions this particular friend, his face beams with delight.

JASON'S ENLIGHTENING MOMENT WITH GRACE

Although Jason was aware that his relationship with Loretta wasn't going well, it took him several months to accept that he actually felt lonelier when he was with her than when they were apart. He was able to recognize that whenever he felt that uncomfortable, empty sensation in his stomach, he was either thinking of her or was with her. The more he desired her, the stronger the discomfort.

Jason's enlightening moment came one evening while sitting with Loretta on a pier with the warm Atlantic Ocean crashing on the pilings below. On this particular evening, everything was ideal for the perfect romantic interlude. He looked over at her as she gazed at the full moon, which had just risen above the horizon. In that moment, he realized that this woman represented every distraction he had ever been attracted to since he was a child. It hit him fully that, in his mind, he was desperately attempting to transform Loretta into his version of the perfect woman. In a flash, he realized how she had been clear with him from the beginning that their relationship was just a stopping-off point for her and not a destination. She was clear that Jason also was her distraction but only for the time being.

Although short in actual time, the moment was complete with a series of snapshots of many of the frustrating times he had experienced as she consistently refused to live up to his expectations. The big difference this time was that there was no self-criticism, denial, and, most noticeably, no need to fabricate another fantasy in an attempt to hide from his emotions. He stood there, totally convinced that he had been lying to himself. Yet he was not devastated; on the contrary, the realization brought a wave of relaxation to every part of his body. As Loretta turned to look at him, it was as if he had never seen her before. It was difficult for him to figure out how he had missed her shallow stare and uncaring glance. His increased awareness in that moment allowed him to completely accept the fact that she did not have any strong romantic feelings for him.

They went to a café close to the pier and, for the next few hours, had their very first authentic conversation. He was keenly interested in discovering things about this woman that he had not once taken the time to find out. He was amazed by her unwavering clarity over not wanting a romantic relationship with him, though a physically intimate one was acceptable to her.

Jason left the pier that evening feeling elated over what he realized were opposite emotions: sadness and relief. The relief came from finally getting clear that his loneliness was something he could not blame on another person. Strangely, he felt ready to deal with his emotions without distractions. Although sobering, the moment was poignant, and he felt stronger in himself.

CAROLINA'S ENLIGHTENING MOMENT WITH GRACE

After her divorce, Carolina wanted to begin dating once again. She was concerned that her choice of men might not match her belief of how a healthy relationship partner should behave. Two of her ex-boyfriends, as well as her husband, had been verbally abusive, leading her to believe that she had a broken chooser—a term we use in our seminars to describe one's subconscious tendency to choose a person who is unavailable to fulfill their relationship needs.

Carolina had completed only a few sessions when she was asked out on a date, which resulted in a barrage of self-limiting thoughts about how she did not feel good enough to start dating again. This was the third person who had asked her out, so she was able to recognize that a pattern was developing: she did not feel she had enough awareness to move forward into the dating world. Although her self-critical thoughts were obvious to everyone but herself, it was only after she began feeling frustrated by not knowing how to respond to these unsolicited requests from the men she was meeting that she was able to acknowledge them herself.

Her distraction for not dealing with her issue was refusing to date.

It was only when she was asked out on a date that she felt so terrible and experienced such fear. Not dating seemed a logical solution to the problem, until she began to study the Frustration Cycle.

Carolina soon became aware that even though her agitation was minor compared to the fights during her marriage, she was in the middle of a pretty big issue activation. The pattern of avoidance was obvious, and now she connected it to her feeble attempt to run away from the inevitable. As is the case with many people, accepting responsibility for her thoughts of *not being good enough* led her to the curiosity stage.

Her enlightening moment came when she gifted herself with a promise to proceed slowly, and the biggest part of her relief came when she decided that she could go on one date and did not have to date the person a second time. Something as simple as that was all she needed to deactivate her issue and allow herself some breathing room to gently dip her toes back into the dating pool.

MICHAEL'S ENLIGHTENING MOMENT WITH GRACE

During an agitating interaction with his newly hired thirty-year-old research scientist, Peter, Michael became aware that he was feeling angry. He thought Peter was discounting his suggestions. Before his work with me he would have just unloaded all of his anger on the employee, which would have eventually resulted in the employee's resignation. This time, however, he recognized the signs that he was getting to the point of losing control: his chest got tight, his jaw was suddenly hurting from clenching it so tightly, and his breath was shallow.

However, with three months of my coaching under his belt, Michael was aware enough to recognize the pattern and avoid his normal method of distracting from his trust issue by criticizing his employee with a barrage of insults. On this day, Michael paused, then grabbed his coat and headed out to the walking trail behind the laboratory. Moving his body briskly along in the cold January air calmed him down enough to remember the conversation he had had with his ex-wife, Jill, three weeks before.

Michael and Jill had had an amicable divorce many years earlier and remained close friends. During their marriage, Jill had tried to make it work well beyond her tolerance level, but finally gave up. Still, she was the only woman Michael had known who was strong enough to counter his negative attitude with love and compassion.

Jill was currently supporting Michael in his work with me regarding becoming more aware of how he kept projecting his corrupt stories onto his workers. In fact, it was Jill who introduced Michael to me and suggested he come for coaching to resolve this problem. Fortunately, Michael was very determined to break his old pattern and take full responsibility for his emotional upsets.

Michael remembered Jill's strong and direct words: "Remember, you are the cause of your employees quitting, because they can't stand working with your relentless criticism." It had been a strong pill for him to swallow, but it was true nonetheless.

Jill continued, "Remember how you used to tell me that you had a better way of doing just about everything?"

On remembering this later, Michael felt himself getting upset, but he knew Jill was right. He went over the entire scene for a few moments when suddenly *it* happened. A feeling of remorse rose up from his chest, hitting him surprisingly hard. He was shocked to feel his eyes moisten and his chest heave as a flood of memories of hurtful things he'd said to Jill filled his consciousness. He wanted to run inside to call her when he realized that what he really needed to do was apologize to Peter and then Jill.

Michael's gift to himself was the thought that he could trust himself to be kind and gentle while setting the appropriate boundaries with his loved ones or employees. As he walked back to his office to hang his coat on a chair, he looked through the blinds at Peter bent over his desk writing something feverishly. It was then that the enlightening moment occurred. He felt thankful that he had chosen this recent graduate from MIT.

Michael walked over to Peter that afternoon, and for the first time in his life, he felt that he could trust this young, intelligent man to perform his tasks and add much to the research paper that was already two years overdue. Peter was new, so he had no idea that Michael's apology was a monumental first step in breaking a very old pattern. Michael did call Jill that evening and shared how surprised he was that trusting someone could feel so good. Jill's response was short and sweet, "I am proud of you, and I could hit you over the head for not realizing that sooner!"

CYNTHIA'S ENLIGHTENING MOMENT WITH GRACE

On yet another hastily arranged business trip to Toronto from Vancouver, an exhausted Cynthia was forced to settle back in her seat and reflect on some uncomfortable thoughts that were bouncing around in her head since the coaching session she had had with me two days before. As the plane continued to climb, even the images on the small video screen in front of her were not compelling enough to pull her attention away from a discomforting yet familiar sensation that something was wrong. She experienced a strong desire to get up out of her seat to walk around the cabin.

Looking up at the FASTEN SEAT BELT sign, she collapsed back into her seat and fell victim to the thought she tried so hard to suppress: *Why am I always attracted to the guys who don't want me?* That was when her issue became fully activated.

Now a flood of memories from her recent ski trip flashed across her mind. She remembered the moment Richard skied past her and was waiting for her as she completed her run down the slopes. She remembered how much she liked Richard during their weekend together; she even relived their meal the evening before she left for her condo in Vancouver. *Why didn't he at least kiss me good night once?*

The thought echoed in her head over and over again. She started to squirm, began to feel claustrophobic and agitated, and her breath shortened—and her old familiar pattern was activated as she thought, *Oh, I forgot to e-mail Sean!*

Without realizing what she was doing, she reached into her purse, grabbed her BlackBerry, and stared down at the blank screen. It was at that moment that she realized the answer to the homework assignment I had given her before she left for this trip: *Discover how you distract from your uncomfortable emotions.*

She sat up stiffly and turned to look out the window at the clouds far below in an attempt to hide her emotions from the older gentleman seated next to her. Yet at the same time, the waves of tears began to moisten her mascara. Cynthia smiled and chuckled as her shoulders dropped, the muscles in her forehead and jaw softened, and deep within her solar plexus a warmth spread up into her chest, as a not-so-familiar voice from somewhere in her mind whispered quietly, *There is nothing wrong with you.*

She let out a deep sigh, relieved and surprised at the same time. Not only was she aware of how painful it felt when she beat herself up for not being good enough to have Richard kiss her at the end of their date, but she was now aware of how she distracted from those feelings. *It's true; Gary told me that not having enough time was the way I distract myself from feeling so worthless inside.* She realized that the simple act of reaching for her BlackBerry was a desperate attempt to push her uncomfortable emotions back down into her subconscious.

It was a half hour later that Cynthia became aware that she was feeling totally okay with doing absolutely nothing. It was unusual, to say the least, for her to acknowledge such a powerful and painful thought without being knocked out of balance. Plus, for the first time that she could remember, she had just spent thirty minutes feeling totally okay and *doing* nothing but *feeling* painful emotions and thoughts.

Gazing down at the snowcapped Rocky Mountains, it dawned on

her that she was experiencing an enlightening moment. She took out her journal and wrote down her issues in large block letters: THERE IS NEVER ENOUGH TIME. THERE'S SOMETHING WRONG WITH ME.

She sat back in the seat and stared down at the words. *There's something wrong with me.* That was the moment she knew without a doubt that she was distracting in a useless attempt to make the pain deep inside go away. *I keep busy when that feeling comes up.* Cynthia had a sudden surge of love for herself as she realized that her compulsion to keep busy was her *distraction.*

MARK'S ENLIGHTENING MOMENT WITH GRACE

After being discharged from the Army Reserve during the recent economic downturn, Mark also found himself without a full-time civilian job. With this double hit, his financial situation was precarious, and on top of that he was also wrestling almost daily with his issue. He kept himself afloat with odd jobs, relying heavily on his pension check, credit cards, savings, loans, and unemployment checks. He became adept at practicing exiting the Frustration Cycle through GRACE.

During a session, Mark shared that he noticed his activations almost immediately because his heart raced, his breathing became shallower, and a wave of panic started to overtake him. Usually he was able to pause, breathe deeply, and call one of his supporters. However, especially during the more severe activations, he still found himself in full distraction mode. This is what frustrated him the most and usually set off a strong bout of *there's something wrong with me.*

He admitted that he was more aware than ever before of his tendency to distract, and he noticed that watching television, indulging in comfort food, and surfing the Internet were all just temporary fixes.

He revealed, "I now catch the distractions early in the process. I am aware of how much energy I have used to run away from the painful feelings of insecurity and fear. However, just about every time

I go unconscious and attempt to suppress the incessant negative mental chatter, I am able to pause and redirect my energy to practice GRACE. However, there are some situations, like dealing with my teenage daughter, that the intensity of the present predicament will trigger all my issues, and that's when it really gets tough."

The intensity of Mark's triple whammy—*no one is there for me, there is something wrong with me,* and *I'm not good enough*—has a sobering effect on him. It's so big that he is forced to notice, remember, and begin the process of getting free (again) from the demoralizing effects of these powerful erroneous core beliefs.

Now when they appear, he is able to move through them, noticing that he is activated, recognizing his patterns of physical, mental, and emotional pain, and accepting full responsibility that his daughters, his financial situation, his being discharged from the army, and all his other distracting thoughts will never bring him to a satisfactory conclusion.

Curiosity, however, is the step that is most difficult for Mark. He, like many others, confuses the fourth step, *becoming curious,* with the second step, *recognizing the patterns.* In the second step, it is essential to recognize the patterns that keep you stuck in thinking that the *situation* is the cause of the upset. Until you can reach the third step, *accepting full responsibility* for your agitation, there is no way of reaching an enlightening resolution to the inner and outer explosions caused by an issue activation.

Mark is now more capable of mastering the *curiosity* step by becoming fascinated by the fact that beneath the surface, hidden and invisible, an emotion is wreaking havoc with his life. He is now more receptive to feel that emotion, to understand it, and to discover as many facets of his fear and loneliness as possible. And he is succeeding because of his diligence, sincerity, and ability to remain strong in his resolve, balanced in his approach, and flexible when his *victim stories* compel him to give up reason and jump on the easier path to distraction.

Mark feels a deep affiliation for his religious beliefs. The manner in which he is now able to replace the pain, distractions, and sense of hopelessness that comes with his issue activations is unique and completely connected to his Christian faith. His *gift,* the one that leads almost regularly to an enlightening moment, is powerfully simple: "Whenever money and job prospects begin to simmer below the surface of my mind, I can see how they activate the physical tension in my body. These are the telltale signs that something is brewing and needs my immediate attention. These obvious culprits remind me to begin my breathing exercises and focus my mind on a favored passage from the Bible, 'Look at the birds of the air, for they neither sow nor reap nor gather into barns; yet God feeds them. Are you not more valuable than they?' This is how I gift myself. It eventually allows the fear, loneliness, and self-criticism to completely dissolve and be replaced by a delightful wave of peace. When this prayer works, I experience my entire mind letting go of all negative thoughts, the tension in my abdomen releases, I feel blessed, thankful, and, most important, inspired to get back into my life, continue my job search, give hugs to my girls, and sit back relaxed, knowing that everything has purpose and meaning in my life. Whatever is going to happen next, I have the strength, flexibility, and balance to deal with it in an aware and intelligent manner. That is my enlightening moment."

WILLIAM'S ENLIGHTENING MOMENT WITH GRACE

It was a Saturday afternoon and William was celebrating a full month of being off his high blood pressure medication. He looked down at the shopping cart full of healthy food. The fruits and vegetables seemed out of place considering what he used to eat before we had discussed the weaknesses of his body type, but that seemed like lifetimes ago as he now prepared for a special wedding anniversary weekend. Ever since he committed to his daily program of a healthier diet, hatha yoga exercises, relaxation techniques, breathing, and meditation sessions, William's life had made a dramatic change for the better.

His wife, Marla, who had spent ten years absorbing his misplaced anger, was now glad to be the beneficiary of authentic conversations with a man she had believed was lost to her forever, and was thankful to have a husband who looked and acted like the caring, loving man she always knew he was capable of being. When I spoke with her briefly during a call to William, Marla expressed how amazed she was that William had achieved such quick results.

These and other changes had also reignited the romance in their marriage, and William was excited to carry out his plans to celebrate their anniversary. As he stood in line at the supermarket, he was lost in pleasant thoughts when suddenly he heard a harsh voice in front of him that jolted his nervous system with a shot of adrenaline. An angry man in front of him was shouting at the frightened young cashier. William said, "Hey, leave the kid alone."

Before William knew it was coming, the man threw a punch at him that hit him square in the chest. The force of the blow pushed him back into the person standing behind him, and as he regained his focus, he acted out of instinct. William lunged at the man with an outstretched arm, clenching his throat in a death grip and pushed him ten feet till he was pinned against a wall. The man was a foot taller and was at least twenty pounds heavier. Before the stunned man could react, and just as both a policeman and the store manager raced to the scene, William raised a fist, ready to finish the fight with one of his powerful knockout punches.

But he did not. He froze his hand mid-punch with his fist inches from the now-frightened man's face. He stared at the man with a sudden reversal of emotion; almost immediately William's face relaxed, his forehead softened, he lowered his arm, and stepped back. The confusion allowed the police officer and store manager to immobilize the man by pinning his arms against the wall. William just stepped back and immediately began taking deep breaths until his heartbeat began to slow down. During those few minutes, he experienced something he did not have words to describe. The emotion of compassion for the angry man's dilemma flooded his consciousness, something he had never imagined possible: he felt sorry for this sad and agitated fellow.

After receiving numerous thanks from the cashier, store manager, and police, and after deciding not to press charges against the man, William walked out to his car with groceries in hand. He sat in the driver's seat, and for the first time in his life he felt oddly light and peaceful. At first he thought he was in shock; however, after the fifteen-minute ride home, he spent the next hour preparing the anniversary meal, whistling an old tune he was surprised he remembered, and enjoying himself immensely.

William's enlightening moment was sudden and totally unexpected but was a result of practicing his program. He had become more aware of how he distracted himself, and trusted himself to handle potentially dangerous situations by now employing a nonviolent method. Most of all, William felt proud of himself for not getting caught in his old patterns, and the road ahead seemed brighter and filled with possibilities. The next week, he told this story to his medical doctor, a friend of many years who had stitched William's body after numerous fights in the past. Aside from being amazed by the sudden shift in William's attitude, he was equally astounded that William's blood pressure hadn't been affected.

STEPHANIE'S ENLIGHTENING MOMENT WITH GRACE

"The bills aren't getting paid. The paperwork is overwhelming. I can't stand to look at the piles. I just don't know how to do this. I have no idea what it takes to run a business." Stephanie's issue is *I am unacceptable.* This comes out in her as the statement *I am a terrible person,* which causes her to be highly self-critical, even more so than someone with the issue *I'm not good enough.* She engages in behaviors that reinforce her low opinion of herself and downplay her accomplishments.

Stephanie was not prepared for what she experienced when she finally mustered up the courage to stand in front of the mirror before dressing after taking her morning shower. She practiced a technique she had learned in our seminars, allowing her eyes to just take in the reflection in the mirror. This was different than her usual pattern of fixing her attention on one area, then moving on to the next. She rather enjoyed just remaining neutral, permitting the image of her body to be received by her eyes, transmitted to her brain, and then set upon the screen of her mind. What she noticed was a total surprise.

First, because of how aware she was when she set up the experiment, she was able to catch her issue activation immediately. When her mind shouted out angrily, *Look at how you have let yourself go,* she immediately noticed the hunger pangs in her stomach. With no hesitation, she closed her eyes for a moment, practicing the deep-breathing exercise that allowed the slow, long exhalations to expel the carbon dioxide that had immediately caused her to tighten her shoulders and belly upon looking at her overweight body. After her initial shock (she figured she must have gained at least five pounds since she last stood on the scale), she settled down to continue practicing GRACE, the next step of which was *accepting responsibility for the agitation.*

Her first attempt was a failure because she got caught up in her story that because she was working so hard for the past week, her diet had certainly suffered. Then she recognized the conclusion as a story that was more about her weight gain (the situation) than about the agitated reaction. The critical outburst was not about the emotional pain of staring at her overweight body in the mirror, but rather the deep-seated erroneous core belief that shouted, *She is a terrible person!* After clearing up the confusion, instead of beating herself up, she was able to return to confirming how strange it was to see a body that needed some healthy alternatives, and then she immediately got hungry.

After another round of deep breaths, she spoke out loud, "What I need to focus on is the 'A' in GRACE. I accept that the negativity I am experiencing has more to do with my belief that *I am a terrible person* than the fact that I have let my body gain weight." Upon taking total and full acceptance for her issue activation, she threw on her exercise outfit, and sat cross-legged on her bed. The next step was her most difficult: getting curious about something that she had spent her entire life suppressing. It was not easy for Stephanie, yet this day she had a breakthrough.

When she reflected upon the fact that she actually got hungry as soon as she noticed the image of her body, she was astounded. She had fought the phantom-hunger signals for years, but this time it was so obvious that her body was tricking her. She was not hungry for food but wanted comfort from the disturbing erroneous core belief that was activated by looking in the mirror. Now *that* was fascinating.

That realization was her enlightening moment. She could not trust her body nor her mind to accurately interpret information gathered through her senses. That was mind-blowing, to say the least. She now returned to the curiosity step by reflecting on how she would have to become more aware of issue-activated hunger compared to a healthy desire to eat. Instead of beating herself up for being a terrible person who had no discipline, she now felt gratitude for all the hard work and practice that had led her to this moment.

While enlightening moments can be powerful and dramatic at times, Stephanie's big *Aha!* experience was a much-needed infusion of insight about a situation that had plagued her for many years. She spent the next hour doing odd jobs around the house that included opening mail, filing, and paying bills *before* they were due, and then she went outside to exercise. It was a good day for Stephanie.

KEITH'S ENLIGHTENING MOMENT WITH GRACE

Keith woke up early Christmas morning to practice some of the techniques he'd learned in our coaching sessions and to go over the materials in his training folder. He knew his wife would be up very soon, followed by their two boys, who would want to open their presents. He glanced down at his notes on GRACE and thought about how he should practice it more often. He went over the steps in his mind, which was quite fortunate, since he was about to really need GRACE that Christmas morning.

He heard a noise in the family room and went to investigate. Jack, the older of the two boys, was standing by the elaborately decorated tree with a sour expression on his face. Keith guessed that Jack had counted up the presents and realized he didn't have as many gifts to open as his brother Luke.

To assure him that the gift-giving was "even," Keith pointed out that the brand-new bicycle by the tree was his. Jack's look of disgust worsened, and Keith was horrified. He never guessed he'd hear the following words from Jack: "I never wanted a bike."

Keith later reflected that without that quick reminder session in his office, he may not have had the foresight to pause and take a breath. Instead, he would have berated his son for being so spoiled and self-absorbed. In fact, Jack was waiting for his father to lecture him on his deficiencies as a person. Instead, after what seemed like an eternity, Keith was aware that he was agitated, he recognized that this old patterned reaction to being frustrated by his son's self-absorbed style would not get him anywhere, and he did something atypical: he opened his heart, looked his son in the eyes, and said, "I'm sorry your expectations weren't met. I feel bad too."

The father and son just stared at each other for seconds. Keith could see the gears in Jack's mind turning as he tried to make sense of his father's response. That's when the enlightening moment hit them both. Tears welled up in their eyes, and Jack leaped into his father's arms, which was totally out of character for their relationship. Jack told Keith that he really did not want a bicycle. Keith felt sad and realized that he had not been focused enough on his son those past few months to even know what he wanted for Christmas. Just taking that extra moment to avoid going into reaction and feeling the sadness for both of them was a very profound moment for Keith, and he thinks it was for Jack as well.

Keith recalled how I had told him that after the enlightening moment occurs, it is essential to go back to deal with the actual situation. And that is what they did. Together, they decided to take the bike back to the store, and with the refund money, Jack could choose a new gift. The rest of the day was a celebration with family and friends.

VERONICA'S ENLIGHTENING MOMENT WITH GRACE

Veronica's life was at a standstill personally and professionally. She dreaded going into her yoga studio on the days when she would have to interact with her business partner, Linda, which made her very uncomfortable. Linda had assumed the parental role in this unhealthy relationship, and Veronica was the rebellious child, lost in the role of victim. In fact, her biggest distraction was blaming others for her dissatisfaction—in this case, Linda. Veronica was suffering from back pain, headaches, and constant low energy, which were inconsistent with her healthy, natural lifestyle and attention to yogic practices. Obviously, there was something else going on for her to be so out of balance with her situation.

Veronica was open to learning how she could exit the Frustration Cycle. The first step for her was admitting that something was not right inside her. This took a while, but when she realized that she had the ability to end the frustrating relationship, she was able to relax around Linda. She finally understood that she was using blame to distract from the emotional turmoil that got reactivated every time she concluded that someone (in this case, Linda) was not listening to her.

As she became more aware that there was a solution to her dilemma, she became curious about how to accomplish it as soon as possible. She was finished with feeling this way. She began to practice being more aware of how often she felt not heard in her interactions with Linda. She began to take notice of the patterns that immediately arose every time her issue was activated. After considerable time and attention, she concluded that it would not be possible for Linda to cause all the physical discomfort in her body and the emotional dis-ease that came up during their business conversations. Becoming more aware of the tension in her chest, the tightening of her lower back muscles, and the tight jaw that began to freeze an angry expression on her face were all important signs of something going on inside of her that were not caused by the situation. When she finally recognized that the painful feeling of being *victimized* by her interactions with Linda was due to her own issue, *No one is listening to me so that must mean that there is something wrong with me,* she was on her way to having an enlightening moment.

Veronica's most difficult step was accepting full responsibility for feeling upset after interacting with her business partner. It took months of practice for her to realize that she was a powerful person who could take full responsibility for every emotional experience in her life. She could not control the situation, but she did have full control over her stories about the situation and her unnecessarily emotional, imbalanced reactions. This gave her hope.

After a while, she recognized her agitated reactions for what they were: a moment of forgetfulness. They became the reminders that there was something else going on inside of her that required her attention. There were many parallels in Veronica's personal life that led her to conclude that her issue was not only activated around Linda. Her personal life was fraught with similar situations and emotional upheavals of the same kind. For now, however, dealing with Linda was a big enough challenge.

Veronica was ready to get curious about how she could find solutions to her problems. This curiosity led to deeper exploration of her own internal state. Soon, she became aware that besides being a mature adult who could handle life, there was often an insecure and frightened part of her that felt no one was listening.

This immature and angry child self felt entirely alone and unrec-
ognized by others. That was the final step in her process as she
reframed her agitation with Linda as originating from a painful emotional place within her own consciousness. It was at that point in her
innerwork that a breakthrough happened for the first time.

During a heated business meeting that was not going the way she
wanted, Veronica realized she was being needlessly argumentative and
unwilling to listen to Linda's concerns about the size of the classes.
Veronica was able to pause in the midst of her internal dialogue about
how Linda did not understand her point, and in that moment she
heard what her partner actually was saying. She even surprised herself
when she told Linda that she agreed with her. The look on Linda's face
was the exclamation point at the end of a surprising response. This
was the first time she had experienced a sense of ease with her partner
in a long time.

In that moment, something was deactivated so quickly that it
took her by surprise. What got her attention most was that she was
not reacting. Later she came to see the enlightening moment had
permitted her to relax, soften her jaw, and have the first authentic
conversation that had occurred in the two years they had been part-
ners. They actually made some important business decisions and
hugged each other as they departed. Veronica knew something big had
happened, because for the next few hours, she had loving, caring
thoughts about her partner.

BETHANY'S ENLIGHTENING MOMENT WITH GRACE

On the days her boss, Joe, visited the store she managed, Bethany
would not eat dinner due to an upset stomach. After some time, she
finally noticed the correlation between Joe's biweekly visits and her
indigestion. She had been practicing GRACE for several months, but
the second step—recognizing the pattern—was quite difficult. Her
journal entries helped her to finally identify the pattern.

For the next few weeks, with this new awareness, she also discovered that her bowels would tighten during Joe's visits, resulting in severe cramping. This was an important realization, and now that it had come to her attention, she was determined to make some changes in her unconscious reactions to her boss's presence. Knowing the schedule of his visits beforehand, she would spend more time practicing her meditation, relaxation, and breathing exercises in advance of his arrival. She was also keenly aware of her body's reaction to Joe, and was therefore able to catch her physical reaction to the situation and avoid the *flight* reaction that had previously defined their relationship. It was a few months later that Bethany had a powerful enlightening moment.

She was in the office when she heard Joe berating the cashier. She had been unaware until then that he had arrived. She knew that there were a few customers in the store. Her stomach began to twitch. She inhaled deeply, left her office quickly, and walked over to the cashier. The customer waiting to be served was clearly embarrassed. Bethany smoothed over the awkward situation while Joe went into the office.

That was when it happened. Watching Joe escape into the office reminded her of her own pattern. Once the customer left the store, Bethany went into the office to have a long and honest talk regarding her discomfort with Joe's unprofessional behavior toward her and her staff. As it turned out, he appreciated her comments.

That evening Bethany felt fantastic. It was the first time in her life that she was able to speak up under pressure and set boundaries. Finding her voice was so exhilarating that she spent the evening sharing the experience with a few friends. Her enlightening moment confirmed what it felt like to feel the fear and move forward anyway. Bethany, of course, reported many more issue activations; however, she also told me that once she had tasted the authenticity and sweetness of being centered and aware in the moment of stress, she had gained the skills of catching her activations sooner and feeling more and more confident in working the steps of GRACE.

APPENDIX B

Gary and Radha's Journey

We are delighted that you've gone on this journey with us.
Now please allow us to share the journey that brought us here:

It was the early 1970s. I was a swami (a celibate monk), and Radha was a married woman. We met in Newport, Rhode Island, where I was lecturing and teaching at our annual ten-day silent yoga retreat with my teacher Swami Satchidananda.* Radha was a participant. Although the paths that brought us to this place were worlds apart, we had somehow arrived at the same destination with the same teacher, inspired by the same yoga philosophy. This was quite amazing, considering I had grown up in a Roman Catholic family in a working-class neighborhood in northern New Jersey across the Hudson River from Manhattan, and I had served as an altar boy in preparation for the priesthood. Radha had been raised as a free-spirited only child living a privileged life in the progressive university town of Princeton, New Jersey, one hour south of New York City.

Upon reaching our twenties, we had both been naturally attracted to the Vedic philosophy, the knowledge of India, as taught in the Yoga

---

*Swami Satchidananda dedicated his life to the cause of peace. He received many honors for his public service, including the U Thant Peace Award in 2002.

Sutras of Patanjali. Each of us, in our own way, had embraced this ancient wisdom with great enthusiasm. While we both followed the teachings of Swami Satchidananda (the founder of Satchidananda Ashrams and the Integral Yoga Institute, a worldwide organization established in 1966), we approached yoga from two different angles that would eventually converge and form the basis of this book.

By the time our paths had crossed, Radha and I had both been through quite a lot of life experience. A hippie by nature, she received her college degree at Goddard College in Vermont, and as part of her studies she had built a unique two-story geodesic dome on a pristine mountaintop in Vermont. She became a founding member of Hunger Mountain Co-op, grew her own vegetables, brewed beer, pressed and froze gallons of apple cider, made her own bread, canned and froze vegetables from a half-acre organic garden, made tofu from scratch, and lived very close to nature. Always seeking and searching for meaning, she met and married her good friend Lee, and on their honeymoon in Morocco she came across the book *Autobiography of a Yogi* by Paramhansa Yogananda. While reading that book, she had an enlightening moment, and her philosophy of life was suddenly transformed into something much greater than even her love of the natural world. Upon returning to her everyday life in Vermont, Radha pursued yoga with a passion, studying everything she could find on the subject. She discovered the book *Integral Yoga Hatha* by Swami Satchidananda and soon became a student of that great yogi who was also famous for opening the Woodstock Music Festival and was the guru for many rock stars of the time. She immediately organized classes and began practicing and teaching everything she'd learned from the many yoga-related teachings she had discovered. It was on her first yoga retreat, after receiving a meditation mantra from Swami Satchidananda, that it dawned on her that she had indeed become a Yogi—not just a practitioner of yoga, but someone who yearned to live and experience yoga for the rest of her life.

Meanwhile, while attending Saint Peter's College, a Jesuit institution in Jersey City, I joined the United States Army Reserve to avoid being drafted after graduation. I wanted my first assignment to include law school. After graduation, with the Vietnam War raging, I received a pair of second lieutenant bars and was given my first assignment: to take a platoon of men into battle in the jungles of Southeast Asia. But a series of life-changing, enlightening moments during my officer basic training had convinced me of the sanctity of all life. I was court-martialed for refusing to use a weapon against another human being, and after four harrowing months, I was somehow given permission to leave the army. After all three army-affiliated law schools rejected my application, and with no job or school in my future, I was introduced to yoga.

Alice was a sixty-six-year-old vice president of a professional employment agency who had just hired me to take over her position, as she was to retire within the year. She and her husband were vegetarians and had spent forty years studying yoga and meditation, which wasn't as widespread then as it is today. Alice took me to my very first yoga class, and like Radha, my life and my worldview were suddenly transformed after being introduced to this practice. I resigned from the employment position after only a few months and moved into an ashram in New York City. After completing a yoga teacher's training course in 1972, I began my career in yoga. It was during those early days of study that I met and became a devout student of Swami Satchidananda. I grew very close to him during this time, was appointed to be on the national board of directors, took pre-monastic vows, and was sent to Montreal, Quebec, to start a yoga institute on behalf of my teacher. These were transformative years, and I benefited tremendously from the personal time spent one-on-one with my dear guru Swami Satchidananda.

It's true that when we met, Radha was married and, by then, I had taken vows of poverty, chastity, and obedience as a celibate teacher. As you can see, this was not your typical story of boy meets girl. It wasn't until two years later, after I had already assisted in Radha's mantra initiation ceremony, that we began to develop a close and trusting relationship in which we could freely discuss our deepest feelings, including our misgivings about our present circumstances. I was devoted to my practices, but after an emotional experience where a throng of Indian devotees threw themselves at my feet during my first trip to India, I had serious doubts about being a Hindu swami. Radha had separated from her husband, Lee, but remained married to him because she didn't know what to do next. As our friendship developed, we assisted each other in dissolving the vows we had taken . . . and, in the process, as destiny would have it, we fell in love, got married, and created a new set of vows.

Our marital vows weren't the typical promises of a new couple beginning their life together. Being yogis, we knew—as we continue to know—that the purpose of human life is to serve the good of all. We agreed that through our union we would serve humanity and make the world a better place in whatever small way we could. We already knew that we had to build our healthy and peaceful marriage before we could help others. And that is exactly what we went on to do.

After seven years of directing my teacher's nonprofit service organization in Canada, and after our first wedding anniversary, we moved back to Vermont, lived in Radha's dome, and started our own nonprofit organization, Essence: Center for Creative Services. I pursued my master's degree in psychology, which drew upon both Eastern and Western theories of psychology and philosophy. It included an around-the-world trip that began with a teaching invitation from the founders of the Findhorn Foundation in Scotland, Eileen and Peter Cady.

For the next nine months, we visited spiritual and psychological centers, accumulating knowledge and gathering information to incorporate into our understanding of how the world functions. Radha supported me both intellectually and spiritually throughout my education, and although I was the one who received the degree, I give Radha much credit for assisting me so devotedly during my studies.

After I graduated, I combined my psychology background with years of studying yoga and meditation (specifically the system of Raja Yoga), an ancient "instruction manual" for mastering the mind. Soon, I was offering courses to health professionals in the medical, business, and psychological fields.

A turning point in my career occurred when I took a two-year training program to become a Hakomi therapist. I studied with the acclaimed psychologist Ron Kurtz. Ron had been the resident psychologist at Esalen Institute in Big Sur, California, in the 1960s and was the founder of the Hakomi Method of experiential psychotherapy, a body-centered therapy that is still a forerunner in the field of holistic psychotherapy. Combining this information with my knowledge acquired while studying and practicing yoga, I developed a therapeutic process that I use with my clients today. I have discovered the importance and relevance of keeping our empathic nature functioning at the highest level with clarity and detachment, which is necessary to navigate life successfully.

In 1979, upon returning from our around-the-world trip, we met Dr. Peter Albright, who was then the president of the American Holistic Health Association of America and keenly interested in starting a holistic health center. As our friendship blossomed, we opened New Directions in Health in St. Johnsbury, Vermont, in 1980. The protocols we developed had tremendous success. Years of working in drug-rehabilitation centers, as well as four hospitals and all of the YMCAs in Montreal, gave me extensive knowledge of how to bridge the gap between yoga and Western medicine. During that time, we developed holistic treatments and various programs that I still use today in my coaching practice.

As both centers thrived, we were busy serving clients and offering classes, weekend retreats, and a residential program. During the 1980s and 1990s, we left both centers in the hands of our trained staff and took yearly three-month sabbaticals and traveled to a meditation center in the Himalayas of India to learn and directly experience the ancient teachings of yoga firsthand. To date, we have visited India eighteen times.

As you might imagine, Radha and I have our ups and downs, as any married couple would over the course of thirty-four years. About ten years ago, while celebrating our twenty-fifth wedding anniversary, we reevaluated our relationship and honestly examined our opportunities and challenges, making important adjustments in how we interact and how we would proceed with our marriage while maintaining our vow to serve others. Through these continuing discussions, we shared many enlightening moments that shone a bright light on the next step for us: it was time to develop our own relationship workshops that would offer unique programs that would seamlessly combine the ancient wisdom of India with the body-mind psychology we had been practicing since 1970. Learning so much over the years, having had so many wonderful experiences, and having succeeded in navigating many trying times, we knew that our next step was to share what we'd learned with others.

Now, nearly forty years since we met, our experiences have led us to this page. In keeping with our wedding vows, we have written this book to be of service to the world. This book is the marriage of our combined wisdom.

Through our workshops and programs, Radha and I have successfully created a shortcut for people who want to get more out of life right away without having to spend forty years in practice, study, and integration, as we have done. In developing our relationship programs, we were delighted to discover that participants would leave with a clear understanding of the work they needed to do to achieve the next level in their life. We've been excited to see firsthand the transformation in so many individuals with whom we've had the pleasure of sharing our teachings as well as those in our community who have worked closely with us in developing these techniques. What strikes us as most significant is that our students and clients now have so many more options available to respond successfully to the challenges and opportunities in their lives.

The people who are attracted to our work are conscious individuals—functional, intelligent, spiritual, loving, and caring—who have reached a plateau in their intellectual, psychological, or spiritual pursuits and are ready for the next step and tools of empowerment in the search for "something more." They are determined and prepared to begin the journey to discover what that *more* is. Our "shortcut" gives them workable tools and skills to take into a difficult world, enabling them to discover for themselves where they are meant to go next and to find the means to go there.

It is our hope that this book reignites your life, or that part of your life that isn't working optimally, and that you experience the transformation from discomfort to comfort, from frozen or blocked to liberated, and that all aspects of your life will begin to flourish. If you are successful, then we have fulfilled our purpose—to be of service.

Om Shanti.
May all find peace.
RADHA & GARY

Glossary

For easy reference, we've included a glossary of terms used throughout this book and in our programs.

agitation: A sudden and immediate emotional disturbance and reaction that occurs when an issue has been activated (see *issue activation*), always as a result of a situation that has caused one to feel victimized. This is not the same as having an emotional response to an event—for example, feeling grief for the death of a pet.

awareness: Pure consciousness; that which enables us to perceive and fully experience our thoughts, emotions, and senses as we navigate the world.

balance: A state of being or awareness on the physical, mental, and emotional levels that allows us to stay centered or to come back to center, even when forces push against us.

distraction: Any issue-activated behavior, thought, or activity that diverts one's attention or awareness away from feeling agitation. This results in its temporary suppression, which often exacerbates the issue in the long run.

emotion: A mental state that arises spontaneously rather than through conscious effort and has accompanying physiological and energetic charges.

enlightening moment: An experience of crystal-clear awareness in which there is no agitation or confusion, only harmony and satisfaction, regardless of the surrounding circumstances.

erroneous core beliefs: *See* Issue.

feeling: A physical sensation intertwined with an emotional experience.

flexibility: The ability to remain physically, mentally, and emotionally open and available to the unknown, allowing one to bend, change direction, or bounce back when obstacles are encountered and/or when preferences are not met.

Frustration Cycle: The cycle in which a situation activates an issue that throws one off balance, causing a corrupted story to be created that leads to the need to distract with the sole purpose of suppressing the painful emotion.

gift: A thought, word, deed, event, and/or emotion that temporarily deactivates a self-limiting belief, resulting in an enlightening moment.

GRACE: An acronym for the five-step process for exiting the Frustration Cycle—*get activated with awareness, recognize the patterns, accept responsibility, curiosity,* and *enlightening moments.*

grooves: Self-enhancing or self-limiting pathways or tendencies in the mind formed by repeating the same or similar experiences and activities until they become automatic.

Bello Method: A body-centered body/mind approach created by the authors that allows a client to learn from and take advantage of the physical, mental, and emotional strengths and weaknesses of his or her body type and its corresponding erroneous core belief, thereby enabling him or her to achieve optimum physical, energetic, emotional, and mental health.

issue: An erroneous core belief, also called a self-limiting belief, held at the core of our unconscious mind that lies dormant, like a computer virus, until activated by our thinking or an outside situation. Each person has at least one major issue. Typically, there are one or more minor issues present in the subconscious mind.

issue activation: A state in which one's awareness has become clouded and his or her perception has become corrupt as a result of an erroneous core belief rising to the surface. This interferes with one's ability to accurately respond to a situation or set of circumstances. That results in the inability to accurately perceive a situation, respond in a balanced fashion, and make accurate conclusions as to the nature of the experience. Activation can vary in intensity and tends to have a recurring physical location in the body.

looking glass: A concept in which everything going on inside a person is reflected back at them through their experiences with the outside world. In other words, a person's response or reaction to an event is in direct proportion to his or her physical, mental, and emotional state of balance; also called the *magical mirror.*

patterns: A recurring behavior, activity, or reaction (such as a habit) developed over a period of time that keeps one caught in a repetitive cycle.

pause button: A moment of reflection in which a person withdraws (either physically or mentally) from a situation to consider how best to respond for a positive outcome or resolution.

probe: A statement or action that is used to search or explore a place within the subconscious mind with the intention of bringing a deeper understanding of oneself to the surface.

reaction: An issue-activated emotional explosion.

relationship: A significant connection or similarity between two or more things or people, or any combination.

self-limiting belief: *See* Issue.

situation: A physical, mental, or emotional event or circumstance that when viewed objectively is neither good nor bad.

story: A string of thoughts with varying degrees of accuracy in response or reaction to a situation.

strength: A state of being on the physical, mental, and emotional levels that allows us to remain steadfast, hold our ground, or maintain our focus when necessary if negative forces oppose us.

suppression: The point in the Frustration Cycle in which a distraction has successfully, but only temporarily, covered up one's agitation resulting from an issue activation.

thought: The mental content of the conscious mind used in the process of remembering, analyzing, fantasizing, and making conclusions in an attempt to understand and direct behavior.

three-part breath: A breathing technique employing the full use of the diaphragm to maximize the intake of oxygen and the discharge of carbon dioxide from the body.

victim mentality: A physical, mental, and emotional state in which a person blames the present and past for the problems in his or her life and admits to little or no responsibility.

Suggested Reading

Awareness Heals by Steven Shafarman, Da Capo Press, 1997.

The Art of Loving by Erich Fromm, Harper & Brothers Publishers, 1956.

The Art of Possibility by Rosamund Zander and Benjamin Zander, Penguin, 2002.

Awareness Through Movement by Moshe Feldenkrais, HarperCollins, 1990.

Be Here Now by Ram Das, Crown Publishing Group, 1978.

Bhagavad Gita, translation by Eknath Easwaran, Nilgiri Press, 2007.

The Body Reveals by Ron Kurtz and Hector Prestera, M.D., Harper & Row/ Quicksilver Books, 1976.

Body-Centered Psychotherapy by Ron Kurtz, Life Rhythm, 1990.

Care of the Soul by Thomas Moore, HarperCollins, 1992.

Effortless Mastery by Kenny Werner, Jamey Aebersold Jazz, Inc., 1996.

Emotional Intelligence by Daniel Coleman, Bantam, 2006.

Essential Rumi, translation by Coleman Barks, HarperCollins,1995.

The Family by John Bradshaw, Health Communications Inc., 1988.

Focusing by Eugene T. Gendlin, Ph. D., Bantam Books Inc., 1981.

The Four Agreements by Don Miguel Ruiz, Amber Allen Publishing, 1997.

Getting the Love You Want by Harville Hendrix, Ph.D., Harper Perennial, 1990.

Homecoming: Reclaiming and Healing Your Inner Child by John Bradshaw, Bantam, 1990.

How to Know God, translation by Prabhavananda and Isherwood, Vedanta Press, 1993.

How to Win Friends and Influence People by Dale Carnegie, Pocket Books, 1998.

Love Is Letting Go of Fear by Gerald G. Jampolsky, M.D., Celestial Arts, 1979.

Loving What Is by Byron Katie, Three Rivers Press (Random House Inc.), 2002.

The Mastery of Love by Don Miguel Ruiz, Amber-Allen Publishing, 1999.

Meditation for Enduring Happiness by Michael J. McCarthy, Archangel Publications, 2011

The Peaceful Warrior by Dan Millman, HJ Kramer, 2000.

Personality Types by Don Richard Riso, Houghton Mifflin Company, 1990.

The Power of Now by Eckhart Tolle, New World Library, 2004.

The Prophet by Kahlil Gibran, Alfred A Knopf, 2010.

Raja Yoga by Swami Vivekananda, Ramakrishna-Vivekananda Center, 1970.

Relax for the Fun of It by Allan Hirsh, M.A., Caramal Publishing, Inc., 2002.

Rhythm of Vision by Lawrence Blair, Schocken Books, 1976.

The Road Less Traveled by M. Scott Peck, Touchstone, 2002.

Spiritual Teachings of the Avatar by Jeffrey Armstrong, Atria Books/Beyond Words, 2010.

The Tao of Leadership by John Heider, Bantam Books, 1986.

Train Your Mind, Change Your Brain by Sharon Begley, Ballantine Books, 2007.

Yoga and Psychotherapy: The Evolution of Consciousness by Swami Rama, Rudolph Ballentine, MD, and Allan Weinstuck, PhD, Himalayan Institute, 1990.

Yoga and Western Psychology by Geraldine Coster, Harper Colophon Books, 1972.

Index

percentages of, 81
Issue(s), 65
 avoiding, 81–82
 deactivating, 123, 128, 129–130,
  131
 identifying through curiosity,
  125–126
 suppressing, 102
 transforming relationship with, 144
 See also Erroneous core beliefs.

J
Journaling, 31–32, 126–127

L
Limitations, exceeding, 149
Looking glass, lessons from, 104–106

M
Meditation, benefits of, 27–28
Memory, 17, 49–51
 and attachment to stories, 95–96
Mental awareness, 11, 13
 subconscious programming and, 13
 See also Awareness.
Mental focus, importance of, 27–28
Mental processes. *See* Thoughts.
Mind–body connection, 55
Mind–strengthening exercise, 83–84
Mind
 as a tool, 10
 defined, 17
 diet and. *See* Nutrition, importance
  of proper.
 focusing the. *See* Mental focus,
  importance of.
 grooves in the, 21
 observing the, 17–18, 19
Mock–agitation exercise, 137–138

N
No–story. *See* Blank thought.

Nothing, wave of. *See* Blank thought.
Nutrition, importance of proper,
 24–25

O
Observer, functioning as the, 18, 19, 20
Operating system, virus in. *See*
 Computer analogy.

P
Partnership, 4
Patterns, 88
 attachment to, 99–101
 becoming aware of, 20–21
 distractions and, 96–99
 GRACE step 2 and, 116–118
 in stories, 94–96
 recognizing, 116–118
 situational, 89–94
Pause button, 20–22, 124
Pausing. *See* Pause button.
Pausing for balance exercise, 107–108
Perception, accurate. *See* Accurate
 thought.
Physical activities, 26
Physical awareness, 11, 12
 emotions and, 12–13
 See also Awareness.
Physical health. *See* Healthy body,
 importance of.
Physical sensations. *See* Physical
 awareness.

R
Reacting, act of. *See* Reaction(s).
Reaction(s), 3, 12, 63, 64, 65, 67, 77,
 78, 80, 82, 106, 114, 117, 118,
 132, 134, 141
 awareness of, 20
 See also Issue activation.
Relationship(s), 4
Relaxation technique, 22–23

About the Authors

Gary Bello received his Masters degree in psychology in 1979, followed by postgraduate work in lifestyle counseling and body/mind therapy. He has founded and directed wellness centers in Montreal, Canada, central Vermont, and South Florida. He and his wife, Radha, founded the Essence Meditation Institute in Marshfield, Vermont, a residential facility that provided ongoing stress reduction, breathing, relaxation and meditation classes as well as extensive teachers' training programs.

In 1980, with Dr. Peter Albright, M.D., Gary cofounded New Directions in Health, a holistic medical center in St. Johnsbury, Vermont, that offered individual optimum wellness programs. Based on his years of experience studying and teaching the science of the interaction between the body and mind (psychoneuroimmunology), he has developed a system that utilizes physical postures, exercise, breathing, and relaxation techniques. This method is currently being taught to and utilized by physicians, therapists, and counselors in the United States, Europe, India, and Canada. Gary travels extensively, teaching and lecturing on the science of living a balanced, peaceful life.

Radha Bello received her undergraduate degree in early childhood development in 1970, followed by advanced training in stress management and holistic body/mind therapies. She cofounded and directed Essence Mediation Institute in Vermont, a residential facility providing holistic programs. She created and managed ongoing seminar and retreat programs in India, Bali, and Hawaii. Radha designed and managed programs at New Directions In Health, a Holistic Medical Center in St. Johnsbury, Vermont.

ABOUT THE CARTOONIST

Allan Hirsh, B.Sc., M.A., is a graduate of McGill University and the University of Saskatchewan. He has been a psychotherapist in private practice for more than thirty years. Allan is also a published cartoonist who incorporates humor and play into his workshops. He has created *RELAX FOR THE FUN OF IT: A Cartoon and Audio Guide to Releasing Stress*. He lives in North Bay, Ontario, four hours north of Toronto. Visit www.allanhirsh.com.

About Pacific Horizon Consulting

Pacific Horizon Consulting offers a premier coaching experience that integrates Eastern wisdom and Western body-centered psychology to enable clients to discover how to live to their fullest potential. In a culture dominated by distractions of every kind, we are prevented from experiencing deep fulfillment. This growing sense of dissatisfaction is the underlying cause of mental agitation, physical discomfort, and many forms of disease.

At Pacific Horizon Consulting, we are acutely aware that people are unhappy and dissatisfied simply because they lack the tools and training to maneuver through life's challenges. Our methods allow clients to discover and change the patterns of behavior and beliefs that prevent them from experiencing a sense of peace, health, fulfillment, and maximum success.

PACIFIC HORIZON CONSULTING
www.pacifichorizonconsulting.com
Email: info@pacifichorizonconsulting.com
Canada: 604.637.4450
USA: 561.404.7226

Audio & Video Offerings
by Gary Bello

To purchase these products, visit pacifichorizonconsulting.com, and click on the PRODUCTS tab.

AUDIO (CDS AND MP3S)

Why Believe Your Thoughts

Learn about the mind and how it functions. The mind analyzes, remembers, and perceives differences. Learn how you should not necessarily accept the contents of your mind as truth.

Guided Meditations

A 60-minute program that includes instruction and guided meditations. For beginners and those with a regular mediation practice.

Relaxation

A relaxation technique that teaches you how to observe your body, mind, and emotions resulting in more awareness when challenging situations arise in your life.

The Solution: Transcending Pain and Suffering

Learn how to recognize, understand, and transform the distractions in your life.

Breath of Life

Experience the effects of the ancient yoga breathing exercises that promote health, relaxation, and a calmer mind.

VIDEO (DVDS)

Yoga for Golfers

A 26-minute instructional program offering simple yet effective exercises and breathing techniques that will enable you to lower your handicap, hit the ball further, and improve course management.

A Healthy Back: You Deserve One

A 30-minute instructional program offers techniques developed from years of experience with medical doctors, physical therapists, and other health providers. Increase the flexibility, strength, and alignment of your back through non-strenuous yoga techniques, breathing, and relaxation exercises.

Yoga—Stretch, Tone, and Relax

A 30-minute instructional yoga program designed to increase flexibility, balance, and strength.